Working with Involuntary Clients

Working with Involuntary Clients

A guide to practice

Chris Trotter

SAGE Publications
London • Thousand Oaks • New Delhi

First published 1999
by Allen & Unwin
9 Atchison Street
St Leonards NSW 2065
Australia

SAGE Publications Ltd
6 Bonhill Street
London EC2A 4PU

SAGE Publications Inc
2455 Teller Road
Thousand Oaks, California 91320

SAGE Publications India Pvt Ltd
32, M-Block Market
Greater Kailash – I
New Delhi 110 048

British Library Cataloguing in Publication data

A catalogue record for this book is
available from the British Library

ISBN 0 7619 6332 4
ISBN 0 7619 6333 2 (pbk)

Library of Congress catalog record available

Typeset in 10.5/12 pt Bembo by DOCUPRO, Sydney
Printed in Singapore by South Wind Productions

Contents

Acknowledgements

THIS BOOK OWES much to William Reid's work on task-centred casework and to Don Andrews' work on pro-social modelling. Whilst they come from different perspectives their publications have provided the inspiration for much of my own research and for much of the material contained in this book.

In writing the book I have been assisted by a number of people. Elizabeth Weiss from Allen & Unwin saw the potential of the book at the outset and has helped to make the process of producing it a painless one. Lesley Hewitt, Michael Clanchy and Jan Mumford provided valuable comments on the early drafts. Lloyd Owen and Colin Roberts gave me very helpful advice on the final draft. I also wish to acknowledge Susan Conran, Julie Chambers, Carmel Laragy, Rosemary Sheehan and the many other colleagues, students and welfare professionals who provided me with case examples and who helped me develop the ideas and practices which are outlined in the book.

Finally, thank you Joan, David and Rebecca for believing in me and for your ongoing support.

1 | Introduction

How do you help someone who has no interest in being helped? What can you do with clients in the welfare or justice systems who are not motivated to change? How do you counsel someone who does not even recognise they have a problem? How do you work with someone who has a totally different set of values from yourself? How can you help someone with their problems and at the same time exercise authority over them?

These are questions which workers with involuntary clients face on a day-to-day basis. Such workers are asked to help clients who have not chosen to be helped and who may be resistant or even openly antagonistic to the assistance they are offered; to help clients and at the same time collect information which may subsequently be used against them; to testify against clients in court and then to work with them in a helping relationship; and to work in a collaborative manner and yet make authoritative decisions about the lives of their clients.

This book aims to help workers with involuntary clients come to terms with these issues.

WHO ARE INVOLUNTARY CLIENTS?

An offender visits a probation officer; a mother is visited by a child protection worker following an anonymous report of child abuse; a drug user attends for drug treatment under the direction of a court order; a man who has abused his wife attends domestic violence counselling at the direction of a court; a psychiatric patient who is a danger to herself and others is offered treatment; a young

1

person living on the streets agrees to go to a refuge with his youth worker knowing that the alternative is to be taken to the police; or a child is placed in a children's home despite the protestations of the parents.

These are examples of involuntary clients. The clients (or recipients of welfare or legal services) in these examples can be described as involuntary because they have not chosen to receive the services they are being given. In fact these clients might be actively opposed to receiving the service. They might believe that it is unnecessary and intrusive. The clients receive the service offered either because of a court order or the threat of some other legal sanction. These clients are sometimes referred to as mandated clients (Rooney 1992; Ivanoff et al. 1994).

The clients in these examples are clearly involuntary. In many instances, however, the distinction between voluntary and involuntary clients is not clear. In the following examples the clients are not required by a court order or even the threat of a court order to receive services; however, their participation is motivated by pressures other than their own desire to address their problems: a mother whose child has been removed by child protection services seeks assistance from a family counselling agency to help get her child back; a drug user seeks rehabilitation counselling prior to a court appearance; an abusive man seeks anger management counselling in response to his partner's threats to leave; or a pregnant teenager visits a counselling agency at her parents' insistence. These clients are partially voluntary and partially involuntary.

Others who receive casework services are more obviously voluntary: for example, a student who seeks assistance from a student counsellor; a couple who seek relationship counselling; a parent who seeks assistance with children who are out of control; or an alcoholic who seeks assistance from a drug rehabilitation centre.

There are, however, aspects of work with clients who choose to receive services which may be involuntary and aspects of work with court-ordered clients which may be voluntary. For example, a student who seeks the assistance of a student counsellor might feel compelled to do so in order to pass her course, or an individual might attend marriage counselling as a result of pressure from her spouse. To give another example, a probationer might visit his probation officer on a voluntary basis in order to discuss problems with his personal relationships.

The distinction between voluntary and involuntary clients is not therefore always clear. It is perhaps best viewed as a continuum, with court-ordered clients toward one end, partially voluntary clients in the middle, and clients who seek services on a voluntary basis toward the other end.

This book is about work with clients who fall at the involuntary end of the continuum. Its particular focus is on work in the community with involuntary clients in areas such as probation (or community corrections) and child protection. Few clients in these settings are voluntary or even partially voluntary. Nonetheless, many of the practice principles outlined in the book also apply to work with involuntary clients in institutions such as prisons, children's homes and psychiatric hospitals. In many cases the principles are also relevant to clients who might be described as partially voluntary or even voluntary.

Both men and women work with involuntary clients, and they work with both male and female clients. For the sake of brevity some chapters in this book refer to the worker as female and the client as male. In other chapters this is reversed.

THE DUAL ROLE OF WORKERS WITH INVOLUNTARY CLIENTS

For the most part workers with involuntary clients work in the welfare or legal systems for government departments or for agencies funded by government departments. They generally have two roles, a legalistic, or surveillance, role and a helping, therapeutic or problem-solving role.

A probation officer, for example, has a responsibility to ensure that a probationer carries out the requirements of the court order. The probation officer is required to take action if a client fails to report or fails to comply with some other condition of the probation. The probation officer might have to report to a court about the progress of the probationer. Simultaneously the probation officer works toward the rehabilitation of the offender by assisting with problems which may be related to the offending behaviour.

Similarly, a child protection worker has the dual task of investigating levels of abuse, taking action to protect a child and possibly taking action leading to prosecution of a perpetrator of abuse, and, at the same time, assisting the family with problems which may have led to the abuse.

Reconciling the legalistic and helping roles in work with

involuntary clients can be a difficult task. It is difficult for a worker to fulfil a helping role with a probationer when that worker is also taking action to have a probation order cancelled. Similarly, it can be difficult to fulfil the legal role where a close helping relationship has developed between the worker and client. A child protection worker, for example, who has worked with a family on a voluntary basis for a period of time may find it difficult if she suddenly has to take action to remove a child.

Coming to terms with this dual role is one of the greatest challenges in work with involuntary clients. Often workers and organisations find it easier to focus on one of the roles to the exclusion of the other. There are examples of workers with involuntary clients who focus almost exclusively on the legalistic role and other instances where they focus almost exclusively on the helping role (Thorpe 1994; Trotter 1996b).

This issue is addressed throughout the chapters of this book. The book aims to assist workers to achieve an appropriate balance between the two roles.

DIRECT PRACTICE

The focus of this book is on direct practice with involuntary clients. It refers only incidentally to community development, policy development and management. It is about the direct day-to-day work with individuals and families which is done by probation and parole officers and child protection workers. As I said earlier, the practice principles discussed in the book are also relevant to workers who work with other involuntary clients, for example, workers in psychiatric clinics, drug counsellors, youth workers, school welfare staff, domestic violence counsellors, family support workers, family counsellors and workers with the aged.

The terminology used to describe direct practice work in welfare and corrections settings has changed over the years. In the 1970s and 1980s the term 'casework' was popular; however, terms such as 'direct practice' or 'clinical practice' are more popular today.

Workers with involuntary clients are often described today as 'case managers' rather than 'caseworkers'. To some extent this change in terminology reflects a change in the way the work is conceptualised and carried out.

The definition of direct practice workers as case managers rather than caseworkers is seen by some recent writers as problematic (Hough 1994; Markiewicz 1994; Ife 1997). They argue that government department staff are increasingly being given responsibility for case management and planning, with problem solving or therapeutic services being left to often under-funded voluntary organisations. They argue that the clients are more and more likely to be managed rather than helped.

The following case example in the area of child protection illustrates the differences between case management, problem solving or therapeutic work and case planning—another term which is often used. A case plan involving a direct practice worker is developed which specifies where and with whom an abused child is to live, how often and in what circumstances that child will have access with natural family members, and what welfare services will be offered to the child and family members.

Following the development of the case plan, the client or client family is case managed. This involves a case manager coordinating the various professionals involved and ensuring that the case plan is carried out. The case management might be undertaken by a worker involved in the case planning or by another worker.

Individual problem-solving work with the client may then be done by another worker. This work might involve, for example, working on problems in the relationship between family members or helping a child to deal with problems at school.

Each of these functions, case planning, case management and problem solving can be viewed as part of the direct practice process. This book focuses on these three functions as a holistic endeavour. It defines direct practice as incorporating each of these functions. Nonetheless each of the three aspects of direct practice is addressed and the framework for effective work with involuntary clients presented here is likely to be useful for those with responsibility for only part of the direct practice process; for example, where the worker has a role exclusively as a case manager or planner, or where the worker has responsibility for therapeutic or problem-solving interventions without responsibility for coordination and planning.

SOURCES OF KNOWLEDGE IN WORK WITH INVOLUNTARY CLIENTS

There is a wide range of theories which influence welfare work with involuntary clients, including, for example, psychoanalytic theory, ego psychology, systems theory, behaviourist theory, human development theory, labelling theory, feminist theory, differential association and modelling theory.

Work with involuntary clients is also influenced by practice models originating from a range of theoretical frameworks, for example, task-centred casework, ecological systems models, transactional analysis, solution-focused models, cognitive behavioural models, rational emotive therapy and a number of different family therapy models.

Work with involuntary clients is also influenced by research findings. For example, workers might be aware of research which suggests that peer group influence can impact on young offenders (Akers 1994), or that working with client goals is more likely to lead to positive outcomes than working toward goals set by the worker (Trotter 1995a).

In addition to theories, practice models and research findings, workers may be influenced in their day-to-day work by their own values and beliefs: for example, that siblings should remain together wherever possible; that women deserve more than they often get in family situations; that marijuana is harmless; that the legal system is unfair; that offenders should be treated more harshly; or that the nuclear family is the best environment in which to raise children.

Workers may also be influenced by particular life experiences, both professional and personal. A case example illustrates this point. A worker in probation confronted a probation client with the reality of his life situation. She said that she believed the client was wasting his life and should be actively seeking work. The client committed suicide shortly after. The experience left the worker very cautious about confrontation with clients.

Workers are also influenced by accumulated life experience, sometimes referred to as practice wisdom. A worker may have worked with young homeless people for many years. She may have found that she is able to relate to these young people better if she has supported the young person through a critical incident in which the young person is distressed, for example following an argument with a family member. Her experience leads her to try to be available to other young people on such occasions in order to build her relationships with them.

Workers are also influenced by organisational expectations and norms. Organisations can have a culture which pressures individual workers to behave in a certain way. For example, in one organisation in which I worked the culture was to see clients as soon as possible even if they arrived without an appointment. This was viewed as respectful. In another organisation the culture was to expect clients to make an appointment for another time. This was viewed as helping clients to be responsible.

A discussion about sources of knowledge is perhaps not complete without some reference to postmodernism. There has been a plethora of literature on the subject in recent years and a number of academics and direct practice workers are influenced by postmodernist thought. Postmodernism offers a different perspective on ways of knowing and sources of knowledge.

Postmodernism is difficult to define; however, Cath Wood (1997) suggests that the concept is characterised by the notion that there are no universal truths and no objective realities. It highlights uncertainty and subjective reality. It focuses on deconstructing the meaning of events and discourses. It suggests there is no one best way to do something. Knowledge is developed through analysis of discourses and narratives. Postmodernism rejects many of the traditional sources of knowledge referred to in this chapter.

The relevance of postmodernism to work in welfare settings is controversial. Some writers suggest that it allows for alternative ways of looking at disadvantage and can 'empower social workers to seek many and varied solutions' (Ife 1997:88). Others point to its failure to take a stand on moral values (a point conceded by Jim Ife (1997) also). Cath Wood (1997) suggests that postmodernism ultimately sees all behaviours as acceptable.

For reasons argued later in this chapter this book focuses more on traditional sources of knowledge such as research findings and values.

THERE ARE THEREFORE many sources of knowledge for work with involuntary clients. Workers often have difficulty identifying how the different sources guide their work. I have conducted many workshops for direct practice workers over the years and have been consistently struck by the difficulty workers have articulating the sources of knowledge on which they base their work. A number of research studies have raised the same difficulty (e.g. Carew 1979; Ryan et al. 1995). This hardly seems surprising given the maze of theories and models, values and beliefs, research findings and organisational expectations which inform the worker's practice.

In work with involuntary clients, where value differences between worker and clients are likely to be accentuated, where the use of authority places particular demands on workers, where client motivation levels are likely to be low and where the development of the casework relationship can be problematic, sorting through the conceptual maze of theory and practice can be even more difficult.

EMPIRICAL PRACTICE

In an attempt to make some sense of this conceptual maze of theory and practice, this book outlines a framework for practice which is based on the research about what works. It presents an empirical practice model.

What is empirical practice? William Reid (1992:7) suggests that empirical practice 'gives primacy to research-based theories and interventions'. He also suggests that empirical practice may involve practitioners carrying out single case study evaluations on their own clients. Others, such as Scott Briar (1990), provide more detailed definitions. The definition I favour and the one which is utilised in this book views empirical practice simply as *the use of research findings as a primary source of knowledge for practice*. This is not to say that research findings are the only source of knowledge for practice, or that theories, values or organisational expectations, for example, are not important. It is simply to say that research findings should be viewed as a primary source of knowledge.

Empirical practice involves a worker having knowledge of research findings in relation to the various practices in her particular field. For example, a probation officer might make a decision about what type of community work placement she will refer a young offender to, taking into account knowledge about studies of the impact of association with other offenders on community worksites (Trotter 1995b). A worker in child protection might be familiar with research which suggests that children are less likely to be removed from families if the worker focuses on specific and achievable client goals (Smokowski & Wodarski 1996). The worker might therefore choose to work with a client to find relief child care for a mother rather than immediately address concerns about her use of drugs.

Criticisms of empirical practice

Critics of the empirical approach argue in favour of practice wisdom, intuition and more qualitative research which focuses on individual experience (see Ife (1997) for a detailed criticism of empirical approaches). Critics suggest that it is reductionist. Because the focus is on measurable outcomes, factors which are not easily measured are ignored. Value-based objectives such as empowerment and social justice, or more individual objectives such as the development of self-esteem, are not pursued simply because they are not amenable to measurement.

For example, a problem-solving or mediation approach to family work might be successful in reducing family conflict. However, such an approach might maintain a patriarchal or even abusive family structure. The work undertaken with the family might therefore achieve one of the goals of the intervention, reduced conflict, but not another more value-based goal—for the family to interact in a more equal manner.

Critics also argue that the empirical approach leads to the notion that there is one best answer and that it downplays diversity. As well as ignoring the objectives which are hard to measure, it often ignores the unspoken objectives which underlie many programs. There are many examples of this.

Most empirical work in corrections rests on the assumption that the purpose of corrections programs is to reduce reoffence rates or to divert offenders from prison. Similarly, empirical work in child protection often rests on the assumption that the aim of child protection services is to enhance the safety of children and to help children to remain with their natural families. However, in reality workers work with a complex syndrome of sometimes competing objectives. An example from probation illustrates this.

A probation officer may have as one objective helping clients to become more law abiding, in other words rehabilitating offenders. However, the probation officer also has an objective of supervising a court order. This could involve, for example, directing clients to community work where they are required to work with other offenders. This might mitigate against the achievement of the rehabilitation objective, given the potential contaminating effects of association with other offenders on community worksites (Trotter 1995b).

The probation officer may also be required to administer a punishment. The client, the courts, the community, and the probation officer herself may see probation as involving in part a level of deprivation of the offender's liberty. Again this may not be consistent with the rehabilitation objective. For example, some research suggests that low-risk offenders are likely to reoffend less if they receive minimal levels of supervision (Andrews et al. 1990); however, the need to offer a certain level of sanction in response to an offence might require a higher level of supervision.

The probation officer may have a number of other objectives, for example, working well within a team, achieving early promotion to a more senior position, or attempting to promote a greater level of justice within the organisation. Again the pursuit of a rehabilitation objective can be inconsistent with achieving these aims. The team may have a more punitive orientation and workers might be rewarded with promotion for fitting in with this punitive approach.

Or to change the example again slightly, research suggests that high-risk offenders (unlike low-risk offenders) are likely to reoffend less if they receive higher levels of supervision (Andrews 1990); however, this might conflict with the worker's objective of facilitating justice. Disadvantaged groups of offenders might effectively receive higher penalties (through higher levels of supervision) because they share risk characteristics such as homelessness and lack of family support. This results in higher penalties for social disadvantage—a clear injustice.

The complexity surrounding the purpose of work with involuntary clients is not limited to corrections. A child protection worker, for example, might aim to reduce the incidence of abuse among clients, however she may also have an objective of avoiding negative publicity. The child protection worker might therefore be reluctant to leave a child with his natural family during an assessment period because of the fear of negative publicity if the child were further injured; even though the worker may be aware of research which suggests that alternative placement may not lead to better outcomes for the child (Gough 1993).

In addition to the confusion at an individual worker level there is often confusion about purpose at an organisational level. For example, there is some evidence that the actual intent behind at least some corrections programs is to punish rather than rehabilitate offenders, despite public expressions to the contrary (Trotter 1996b). There is also some evidence that whilst the intention of child protection services may be to reduce abuse, in practice the system does little to reduce abuse (Gough 1993). Senior managers in child protection services may sometimes be more concerned about public perceptions of their competence than improved outcomes for families. This confusion about objectives at an organisational level inevitably makes it more difficult for direct practice workers to be clear about their objectives or purpose.

In short, workers with involuntary clients have multiple objectives. These are sometimes hard to measure and may not even be articulated by the workers themselves or their organisations. Empirical practice, however, tends to focus on a narrow range of objectives, apparently ignoring many of these other objectives. Yet this book presents an empirical practice model. Why is this?

Advantages of empirical practice

Proponents of empirical practice argue that in work with most involuntary clients there is a presenting problem which leads the client to become a client. The problem may be offending, neglect or abuse, self-harming behaviour, violence within marriage, or one of many others. Empirical practice is based on the view that it is important that this presenting problem is reduced or alleviated.

Research about how such presenting problems have been dealt with in the past and which approaches have worked best can give workers knowledge to guide their practice and lead to improved outcomes—that is to less offending, abuse, violence, or self-harming behaviour.

For example, research in probation informs us that supervision which simply focuses on the development of the relationship between worker and client is not generally related to reduced client reoffending rates (Andrews et al. 1990; Trotter 1996a). On the other hand, a focus on reinforcing client pro-social expressions and actions in probation supervision *is* associated with reduced reoffending (Andrews et al. 1979, 1990; Trotter 1996a).

An approach to supervision which is informed by knowledge of this research (an empirical approach) is more likely to lead to reduced reoffending. Whilst probation supervision has objectives other than reduced offending, if reduced offending is in fact one of the objectives, it seems hard to justify an approach which does not make use of research about how best to achieve it.

Empirical research is indeed more likely to focus on specific outcome measures, such as client satisfaction with service, reoffending or further abuse, and to ignore objectives which are hard to measure, such as social justice, self-esteem or emotional wellbeing. It seems to me, however, that this represents an argument for developing ways of measuring social justice, self-esteem or emotional wellbeing (if these are program or worker objectives) in order to examine the extent to which interventions are successful with them. The alternative seems to be to simply ignore whether or not programs or interventions are achieving what they set out to achieve. Hardly an optimal approach.

Similarly, the argument that empirical practice is inappropriate because it focuses on limited objectives and does not address the often unspoken objectives of workers seems flawed. Again this criticism is not so much an argument against empirical practice but rather an argument for individual workers and organisations to be clear about what it is that they are aiming to achieve—and an argument in favour of a wider body of research which examines different outcome measures. If, for example, the real aim of a correctional program is to punish or to satisfy a perceived community need to see justice done, then in order to assess the effectiveness of that program a clearer definition of purpose is needed. Empirical practice certainly encourages this.

There is no doubt that empirical practice does not supply all the answers. There are many areas of practice with involuntary clients where insufficient research has been done or where research findings are so equivocal that they can contribute little to day-to-day practice. In many instances, however, research has been undertaken using program objectives which are consistent with at least some of the objectives pursued by workers and organisations. In these instances use of this research can lead to better outcomes for clients (e.g. less offending, less abuse).

Empirical practice involves workers being clear about what they are trying to achieve and making use of research findings in their day-to-day work. It does not deny the existence of values or diversity or the complexity of purpose. In fact, it is argued throughout this book that a conscious focus on values and purpose is vital to effective work with involuntary clients. Empirical practice does not deny the importance of theory. On the contrary, theory is vital in guiding research and explaining research findings. Empirical practice simply recognises that research allows us to learn from past experiences and should therefore be a primary factor in guiding work with involuntary clients.

PURPOSE OF THIS BOOK

This book aims to present a framework for practice with involuntary clients which is based on research about what works. It aims to present a framework which makes some sense of the multiple sources of knowledge which workers use on a day-to-day basis in their work with involuntary clients. The book also aims to present this material in a way which is user friendly. As I have said, it does seem that workers have difficulty both articulating and utilising the various sources of knowledge about their work with involuntary clients, and my aim here is to present the material in such a way that it is readily translatable into the day-to-day work situation.

By influencing those who work with involuntary clients, I in turn hope to influence outcomes for those clients. I am hopeful that this book can contribute something to the lives of the offenders, the abused women and children and others who might receive services from the readers of the book.

Two other texts focusing on involuntary clients have been published in recent years, *Strategies for Work with Involuntary Clients* by Ronald Rooney (1992) and *Involuntary Clients in Social Work Practice* by Andre Ivanoff, Betty Blythe and Tony Tripodi (1994). This book is different from these books in several ways. Unlike the others, this book presents a specific integrated intervention model for work with involuntary clients which has been developed from the empirical research about what works, and which has been shown to be successful in the author's own research. The model presented here has a particular focus on issues of role and on a pro-social approach, in contrast with the other books. This book also focuses on work undertaken with involuntary clients by workers with various academic backgrounds rather than focusing specifically on social work practice.

Structure of the book

Chapter 2 summarises the theories and research about what works and what doesn't in work with involuntary clients. It refers to my own research carried out with offenders and families. Chapter 2 outlines the research basis for the following chapters and it is therefore central to the book. The following chapters offer a summary of the research material so that each one can stand alone. This leads to some level of repetition, however it will save the reader the trouble of having to regularly refer to Chapter 2 to understand the research context.

Chapter 3 discusses clarifying the role of the worker. It addresses the dual roles of helping and of social control, and the different perceptions of role from the point of view of senior managers, workers and clients. It also identifies role-related issues which might be discussed between workers and clients. Case examples are used in this and subsequent chapters to illustrate the practice principles. Where these are actual examples the details are changed so the clients cannot be recognised.

Chapter 4 presents a framework for dealing with situations where workers and clients have different values and goals. It presents a method of encouraging more pro-social values. It also considers how culture and gender impact on both client and worker values and goals.

Chapter 5 outlines a problem-solving process for work with involuntary clients, including a framework for case management, case planning and the use of community resources.

Chapter 6 examines the worker–client relationship and the place of empathy and other interpersonal skills, including self-disclosure and humour, in work with involuntary clients. Chapter 7 proposes a method for working with family groups where one or more members of the family is an involuntary client. The final chapter, Chapter 8, considers how workers might evaluate their own practice.

2 | What works and what doesn't?

DO OFFENDERS OFFEND less as a result of the work their probation officers do with them? Are children safer as a result of the work which child protection workers do with families? Do drug users use less drugs as a result of casework intervention? Are mental health patients less likely to be readmitted to hospital if they have a case worker to assist them? Do involuntary clients benefit from casework?

Researchers have been attempting to answer these questions for many years. In fact the research into the effectiveness of work with involuntary clients has a controversial history. The early studies were pessimistic.

One of the most well-known reviews of the effectiveness of casework was undertaken by Joel Fischer in 1973. This review of research looked at the effectiveness of casework services offered by qualified social workers in the United States in a variety of fields, including juvenile corrections, schools, families and the elderly. Each of the studies had a control group and considered outcome measures such as court appearances, teacher ratings of students' behaviour and family functioning. Whilst the review did not specify which of the studies were undertaken with involuntary clients, an examination of the study samples suggests that more than half were involuntary (e.g. five of the eleven studies reviewed focused on delinquent or 'pre-delinquent' young people).

Fischer concluded that 'lack of effectiveness seems to be the rule rather than the exception' (1973:376). However, whilst he found that casework services overall were ineffective, he argued that this disguised the fact that some clients benefited from services and some deteriorated as a result of the services. In other words, it was not so much that casework services had no effect but that they had both beneficial and harmful effects—casework services could be for 'better or worse'. For example, some offenders offended more and some offended less after they were given casework services.

This theme has run through the research about effectiveness since that time. Hundreds of studies have pointed to the idea that some things work and some things don't. There are some casework or direct practice approaches which lead to better outcomes for most clients whether voluntary or involuntary and there are some approaches which fairly consistently lead to poorer outcomes (e.g. Reid 1997a).

Obviously the direct practice approach is only one of the factors influencing client outcomes. Outcomes are also affected by the clients themselves and their potential for change, the family or other support available to the client, and the availability of community resources, including, for example, employment opportunities. Nevertheless the casework approach is one factor in the situation that is in control of the worker.

The extent to which the skills of the worker influence client outcomes is difficult to assess. I conducted a study in probation in Melbourne, Australia, which found that worker skill made a difference of somewhere between 20 and 70 per cent to client reoffending rates (Trotter 1996a). Probation officers who made use of the practices identified in the research as effective were half as likely to have clients who went to prison. Similar strong associations between the nature of corrections programs and reoffending are reported in a review by Don Andrews and his colleagues (1990).

As I suggested earlier the 'what works' issue is controversial. Some recent reviews of the research literature continue to suggest that nothing works or at least that many direct practice approaches are ineffectual (Whitehead & Lab 1989; Gough 1993). However, these arguments are receiving less and less favour. The weight of evidence, as illustrated later in this chapter, suggests that direct practice with involuntary clients can be influential—it can lead to substantially improved outcomes, however it can also lead to poorer outcomes.

THIS CHAPTER OUTLINES the direct practice approaches or skills which the research suggests are related to positive outcomes. Effective programs or positive outcomes are defined in different ways in different studies. Effectiveness is defined in this book in terms of improvement in specific outcome measures. These outcome measures relate to the objectives of the program or intervention. For the most part an effective program or intervention is one which leads to reduced incidence of presenting problems, such as child abuse or offending, or perhaps to improvements in client satisfaction or worker assessment of progress. In most of the effectiveness studies reported in this chapter the outcome measures are compared with a control group which has received an alternative intervention or no intervention.

The chapter is divided into discussions about approaches which have consistently been found to be effective with involuntary clients, approaches which have been found to be effective in some situations or about which the research is equivocal, and approaches which the research suggests are ineffective or harmful. An effective practice model is outlined. The relationship between this model and other theories and models is briefly discussed.

In many instances it is unclear whether the research studies relate to voluntary or involuntary clients. In child protection and corrections the clients are nearly always involuntary. However, as discussed in Chapter 1, in areas such as domestic violence, mental health and drug treatment, clients may be voluntary or involuntary. The focus of this chapter is therefore on studies of child protection and corrections clients with some references to studies with other client groups in fields such as youth work, drug abuse, domestic violence and mental health.

APPROACHES THAT WORK

The research suggests that effective work with involuntary clients is characterised by clear, honest and frequent discussions about the role of the worker and the role of the client in the casework process; by the worker focusing on modelling and encouraging pro-social expressions and actions by the client; and by the use of a collaborative problem-solving approach which focuses on the client's definitions of problems and goals.

Accurate role clarification

Outcomes are improved for involuntary clients when workers focus on helping them to understand the role of the worker and the role of the client in the direct practice process. This involves ongoing discussions about issues such as authority and how it might be used, the dual role of the worker as helper and social controller, the aims and purpose of the intervention from both client and worker perspectives, as well as issues relating to confidentiality. In short, clarifying role is about the question: 'what are we here for?'

Don Andrews and his colleagues (1979) examined tapes of probation interviews in Canada and found that probationers were significantly less likely to reoffend if interviews were characterised by frequent discussions about the probation order and clarity about rules and sanctions and how they would be applied.

Lawrence Shulman (1991) in his study in child protection in Canada found that 'clarifying the worker's purpose and role' and 'reaching for client feedback on purpose' were related to a number of outcome measures, including client views about worker helpfulness. A British publication, *Child Protection—Messages From Research*, suggests on the basis of a number of studies that effective work in child protection is characterised by honesty on the part of the worker and clarity about 'what is happening and the options available' (HMSO 1995:46).

Lynn Videka Sherman (1988) undertook a meta-analysis on the effectiveness of social work practice in mental health. Meta-analysis provides an alternative method of reviewing empirical literature. It can be described as 'a method of aggregating and statistically analysing the findings of several studies' (Fischer 1990:297). Whilst Videka Sherman did not specify the extent to which clients were voluntary or involuntary, part of her study did focus on chronically ill mental health patients, many of whom were in the system on an involuntary basis. Videka Sherman found that mental health clients had better outcomes if 'the intervention and the client's role are described clearly and discussed with the client before intervention begins' (Videka Sherman 1988:326).

Jones and Alcabes (1993), in their book *Client Socialisation: The Achilles Heel of the Helping Professions*, argue on the basis of a research review in the areas of child abuse, drug abuse and mental health that client socialisation is the key to effective work. They view client socialisation as helping the client to become a client, or teaching 'those needing help how to become clients' (Jones and Alcabes 1993:xiii). This process involves the worker and client agreeing on the problem to be addressed and the help-seeker learning the role of client before entering a treatment phase. The prospective client becomes a client only when she accepts and understands how the worker can help and what is expected of the client in the process.

It does appear that one of the key skills in work with involuntary clients is the skill of clarifying role. This is addressed in some detail in Chapter 3.

Reinforcing and modelling pro-social values

The research on work with involuntary clients points to the importance of approaches which reinforce and promote pro-social values. Defining 'pro-social' is not a simple task. Defined narrowly it refers to values and actions which are non-criminal. Defined more broadly it refers to values or actions which might be construed as the opposite to criminal. In other words, actions and values which support and care for others, for example, non-violent interaction in domestic situations, equal personal relationships, caring for your children, trying to support yourself financially and not abusing drugs. It refers to values of non-sexism, non-racism, openness and tolerance. Chapter 4 discusses the meaning of the term in more detail and deals with some of the complexities and controversies relating to the pro-social concept—in particular the perception that pro-social values may support the status quo.

The pro-social approach, as it is defined in this book and elsewhere (Trotter 1997a), involves workers identifying and being clear about the values they wish to promote and purposefully encouraging those values through the use of praise and other rewards. It also involves appropriate modelling of the values the worker seeks to promote, and challenging anti-social or pro-criminal expressions and actions.

There is a considerable amount of research which suggests that the pro-social concept is related to improved outcomes with a range of involuntary clients. David Gough (1993) reviewed 23 studies of child protection programs which offered intervention based on the use of social learning theory. These programs involved the 'identification of inappropriate interactions (between parents and children), the re-inforcement of positive interactions and ignoring of negative behaviour' (Gough 1993:125). Gough indicated that these approaches were among the best researched in his review and that they were 'effective in cases of physical abuse' (Gough 1993:9).

John Masters and his colleagues (1987) reviewed more than 70 studies undertaken with a wide range of client groups, some voluntary and some involuntary, which made use of modelling and reinforcement of positive behaviours. Each of the programs studied had successful outcomes on the measures used. The authors point to studies where modelling and demonstrating desirable behaviours have proved effective in changing the behaviour of psychiatric patients, intellectually disabled clients, children with behaviour problems and school refusers.

Jim Barber (1995), in a review of literature relating to work with drug users who are resistant to treatment, also points to the value of interventions which reward and reinforce positive non-drug using behaviours and which confront rationalisations. Barber refers to one study (Miller et al. 1974) which produced substantial declines in consumption among alcohol users when they were rewarded with token payments following zero blood/alcohol readings. Similarly a meta-analysis relating to the treatment of drug abusers by Acierno et al. (1994) pointed to the value of reinforcement of abstinence and behaviours which competed with drug use.

MORE THAN TEN studies in both juvenile and adult probation have pointed to the importance of modelling and reinforcing pro-social values (or a pro-social approach). These are reviewed in Trotter (1990, 1995a). Two particular studies are outlined here.

Don Andrews et al. (1979) examined tapes of probation interviews in Canada and found that when probation officers modelled and reinforced pro-social comments and actions and also made use of empathy and reflective listening practices, their clients offended significantly less often than the clients of other probation officers. Andrews and his colleagues argue that the reinforcement process was only effective when the probation officers also had good relationships with their clients, developed through the use of empathy and reflective listening.

A study conducted in Australia (Trotter 1990) found that volunteer probation officers who were more pro-social had clients who offended significantly less often in comparison with clients of probation officers who were less pro-social. This occurred regardless of the levels of empathy of the probation officers. The measure of pro-social was taken from the California Personality Inventory socialisation scale, previously known as a delinquency scale (Gough 1960).

These findings are largely replicated in a later Australian study (Trotter 1993) which found that more pro-social officers were more likely to use pro-social modelling and reinforcement and were more effective. The details of this study are outlined later in this chapter. The pro-social approach is examined in Chapter 4.

Collaborative problem solving

The research into work with both voluntary and involuntary clients points to the importance of working with a collaborative problem-solving approach. In fact problem-solving approaches have gained wide acceptance in welfare circles and many of the recent texts in social work and welfare concentrate heavily on outlining models of collaborative problem solving (e.g. Reid 1992; Compton & Galaway 1994; Hepworth et al. 1997).

Problem solving involves working with the client's definition of the problem, developing modest achievable goals which are the client's rather than the worker's (or at least collaboratively developed), and identifying strategies with the client to achieve the goals (Reid & Hanrahan 1981; Rubin 1985; Sheldon 1987). Rubin comments in his review of effective casework practices (1985: 474) that:

> These forms of practice [problem solving] were found to be successful with such diverse groups as mildly to moderately retarded adults, chronic schizophrenics in after care, young non-chronic psychiatric inpatients, women in public assistance and low-income children experiencing school problems.

The study I referred to earlier undertaken by Don Andrews et al. (1979) in probation in Canada found a significant correlation between the use of a collaborative problem-solving approach and reduced reoffending by probationers. Problem-solving practices by probation officers were measured by examining audiotapes of the probation interviews. My own work in probation in Australia also found a relationship between the use of collaborative problem solving by probation officers (measured by an analysis of file notes) and reduced offending and reductions in problems reported by clients (Trotter 1993, 1996a).

Shulman, in his study in child protection, found a relationship between partialising client concerns (or specifically defining problems) and positive outcomes. Similarly, Smokowski and Wodarski (1996), in their review of empirical evidence in child welfare, found support for this approach. There is also support for these approaches in mental health (Videka Sherman 1988; O'Hare 1991; Jones & Alcabes 1993; Reid 1997b).

In work with involuntary clients, working with the client's definition of the problem toward client goals can be inappropriate. A sex offender, for example, might not define his offending behaviour as a problem and his goal might be to avoid detection in the future. A schizophrenic client who is required to take medication might view the medication as the problem rather than the anti-social behaviour which occurs when she fails to use it.

Nonetheless the research consistently points to the need to work with client definitions of problems and goals with both involuntary and voluntary clients. In fact problem-solving approaches which work with clear definitions of problems in clients' terms and clear achievable goals have received so much support in the research over the years that they have almost become the social work and welfare method. Problem solving is discussed further in Chapter 5, which considers how a collaborative problem-solving approach can be developed in work with involuntary clients who are often resistant and often have different goals from the worker. Chapter 5 also considers some of the criticisms of problem-solving approaches.

An integrated approach

Outlined below is a brief summary of the methodology and findings of a study I undertook in probation in Victoria, Australia (Trotter 1993, 1995a, 1996a). This study forms the research basis for much of the material presented in this book. For more detailed discussion about the aims, methodology and outcomes of the study see Trotter (1996a).

The study was based on the hypothesis that probation officers who make use of role clarification, pro-social modelling and reinforcement, collaborative problem solving and empathy (discussed in the next section) will have clients who are more likely to experience reductions in their problems and less likely to reoffend than clients of officers who don't make use of these principles.

A group of 30 probation officers was offered a training course in these principles. Twelve probation officers agreed to make use of the principles with their next ten clients. The remaining eighteen did not continue with the project for a number of practical reasons. The study sample was selected using a systematic random method. It consisted of 104 clients in the experimental group—clients of those probation officers who undertook the training and agreed to make use of the model. (A number of clients were excluded from the sample because they transferred to other offices in the first three months of the study.) The study also included a control group consisting of 157 clients selected from the same offices as the experimental group but with different probation officers. A sample of clients of those probation officers who withdrew from the project but continued in the probation service (105) was also followed up; however, the results for this group were very similar to the control group and are therefore not reported here.

Data was collected through a questionnaire to clients and an analysis of client files and police records.

The study found that:

1. File notes suggested that probation officers who completed the training and agreed to use the model were significantly more likely to use the principles compared with the probation officers who supervised clients in the control group. In other words probation officers were more likely to use the principles after training.

2. Clients receiving supervision from those probation officers who did the training and agreed to use the model (the experimental group) were significantly more likely to report that their problems were reduced during the period of probation than clients in the control group. In fact almost twice as many clients in this group reported that their problems relating to drug use were reduced than in the control group.

3. The reoffence rates for clients in the experimental group were significantly lower than for clients in the control group after one and then four years. For example, the imprisonment rate after one year for clients in the experimental group was almost 50 per cent lower compared with clients in the control group. This is illustrated in Table 2.1.

4. The model was most effective with young, high-risk, violent and drug-using offenders.

5. The use of pro-social modelling and reinforcement as revealed

Table 2.1   **Trotter study (1996a) offender imprisonment rates after one year and four years**

	Clients of trained probation officers	Control group
1 Year (p = 0.04)	13/104 (12%)	33/157 (21%)
4 Years (p = 0.02)	27/104 (26%)	61/157 (39%)

in file notes was consistently, strongly and significantly correlated with lower reoffence and imprisonment rates.

6. The use of problem solving was related to reduced reoffending, although it was most influential in improving compliance with the probation order (e.g. keeping appointments and special conditions).

7. The use of role clarification was correlated with lower reoffending but not at significant levels. This may be explained by the tendency of probation officers to discuss issues of role after the probation officer became aware of reoffending.

8. Probation officer empathy as measured by a psychological test and comments in file notes was not related to client reoffence or imprisonment rates. However, judgemental comments in files (e.g. no-hoper, lazy, liar) were related to increased reoffending even when client risk levels were taken into account. Whilst officer empathy was not a factor in client reoffending the extreme lack of it was.

9. The results of the study could not be explained by intervening variables such as frequency of contact between workers and clients, client risk levels, or the experience or education of probation officers.

The methodology of this study is discussed in detail elsewhere (Trotter 1993, 1995a, 1996a) and interested readers should refer to those publications. The results, I believe, are persuasive, particularly given their consistency with the studies cited earlier and the replicatory nature of the study. The results confirm the importance of workers modelling and reinforcing client's pro-social comments and actions, and the use of collaborative problem solving. Whilst the study is less persuasive in relation to role clarification, this seems to have been due to a particular intervening variable. The study does not support the value of empathy, although it does suggest that judgemental attitudes are related to poor outcomes. Empathy and other elements of the worker-client relationship are discussed in the next section.

APPROACHES THAT SOMETIMES WORK

This section outlines approaches to work with involuntary clients which the research suggests work with some client groups and not others, or about which the research is more equivocal.

The worker–client relationship

This relationship is defined by Compton and Galaway (1994) as including six elements: concern for clients; commitment to and acceptance of obligations toward clients; acceptance of the client as a person (as distinct from their actions); expectation or belief that people can change; empathy or understanding of the client's feelings and point of view; genuineness and congruence (or openness and consistency); and appropriate use of authority and power. Other writers offer similar definitions although O'Connor, Wilson and Setterlund (1995) include self-determination. Other definitions of the casework relationship effectively define it as the casework process itself incorporating goals, tasks and termination (e.g. Marziali & Alexander 1991). To some extent the definition of the relationship is individual. In this book the relationship is viewed as incorporating interpersonal skills, such as empathy and reflective listening, self-disclosure, use of humour and optimism. The issues of authority and power, confrontation, genuineness and confidentiality are dealt with as part of discussions about the pro-social approach and role clarification in Chapters 3 and 4.

How do the various elements of the relationship relate to outcomes for involuntary clients?

Empathy
Empathy can be defined as understanding the client's feelings and point of view. Reflective listening is effectively a practical manifestation of empathy. It is a counselling technique which involves responding specifically to the feelings and content of the client's expressions.

It has long been argued that empathy is an essential skill in effective helping (Truax et al. 1966; Carkhuff 1969). Most recent texts in direct practice in welfare settings discuss empathy as an important aspect of counselling or helping work without detailing research support for its effectiveness (e.g. Compton & Galaway 1994; O'Connor et al. 1995; Hepworth et al. 1997).

The research support for the use of empathy in work with involuntary clients is, however, somewhat equivocal. Don Andrews et al. (1979) found that probation officers who scored high on a psychological test of empathy had clients who offended more often than probation officers who scored low on the empathy test.

Similarly, probation officers who made use of reflective listening practices in taped interviews had clients who offended more often.

As discussed earlier in this chapter, however, Andrews and his team also found that if probation officers had high levels of empathy, made use of reflective listening practices and also made use of pro-social modelling and reinforcement their clients offended less often. In other words, when probation officers were pro-social and also had good relationships with their clients the clients did well. On the other hand, when probation officers were less pro-social and more pro-criminal (on psychological tests and in interviews) and also demonstrated high levels of empathy and reflective listening—the clients did worse. In fact they offended nearly twice as often as other clients in the study.

It seems that empathy set the conditions for change; however the direction of that change was dependent on the pro-social attitudes and skills of the probation officer. It seems that the use of empathy in response to pro-criminal comments by probationers gave some kind of subtle permission or sanction for continuing that behaviour with the result that further offending occurred.

My own work on the relative effectiveness of empathy and pro-social approaches in probation in Australia suggests a different conclusion in relation to empathy. In my study volunteer and professional probation officers who had high levels of empathy did no better or worse than probation officers who had low levels of empathy. And pro-social officers with high levels of empathy did no better than pro-social officers with low empathy levels. These studies used psychological tests of empathy (Trotter 1990, 1993) and measurements of the use of empathy in file notes (Trotter 1993, 1995a, 1996a).

However, as mentioned earlier, the one finding that was significant in this study related to the use of judgemental comments. When workers made judgemental comments in file notes (e.g. lazy, no-hoper) clients offended more than other clients even after risk levels were taken into account.

Some work has been done on the use of empathy with other groups of involuntary clients. Andre Ivanoff and his colleagues (1994), cite several studies undertaken with a range of involuntary clients which point to the potential of a genuine, empathic, helping relationship to be overwhelming and even aversive. William Nugent and Helene Halvorson (1995) also found in role-played interview simulations that inappropriate paraphrasing of client comments could elicit anger, anxiety and depression in clients. These authors favour an approach involving the provision of possible alternative interpretations of the client's expressions rather than simply reflecting what the client has said.

On the other hand, Shulman (1991) found a positive relationship between helping child protection clients to manage their feelings and client perceptions of the worker as caring. Helping clients manage their feelings was defined as 'reaching inside of silences, putting the clients' feelings into words, displaying understanding of clients' feelings and sharing workers' feelings' (Shulman 1991:44). Caring workers in turn did better on a number of client outcome measures. They were viewed by clients as more helpful, their clients spent less days in care (away from their parents) and were less likely to go to court.

Shulman's notion of helping clients to manage their feelings is broader than the concept of empathy and reflective listening. This might help to explain the different findings. Nonetheless the research in relation to the value of empathy in work with involuntary clients seems somewhat confusing. There is little doubt that workers with involuntary clients need to be able to understand their clients' point of view in order to work with client goals and definitions of problems. Judgemental approaches seem to be most unhelpful. It may be important, however, that workers also make use of pro-social modelling and reinforcement to ensure that the impact of empathy is positive rather than negative.

Humour

Humour is rarely addressed in the direct practice literature, however there is some evidence that it can be an influential factor in work with involuntary clients. Studies in child protection and corrections have referred to its importance.

Lawrence Shulman (1991), in his study in child protection, found that child protection workers who had a sense of humour (rated by their supervisors) were more likely to be viewed by their clients as helpful, skilful and trustworthy. Their clients also had fewer admissions to care and fewer court appearances. A study by James Alexander et al. (1978) found humour, among a number of other therapist characteristics, to be related to positive outcomes (including reduced reoffending) for young offenders involved in a family therapy program.

David Pollio (1995) argues that humour can be an appropriate tool for the crisis worker with voluntary and involuntary clients. He distinguishes between humour as a conscious technique and situational humour. He suggests that humour that arises from the direct practice situation can be both helpful and harmful, while the telling of jokes is almost always inappropriate. Humour, Pollio suggests, can be used to break an impasse in the casework process and humanise situations. On the other hand, he suggests it can also be demeaning and cause the client to become angry. He encourages the use of humour in situations where the client can understand the humour, where it suits the style of the worker and where it is appropriate to the situation.

There is clearly a need for more work in this area. It does seem, however, that in the meantime workers with involuntary clients should not be afraid of the use of humour in their day-to-day work. It may help to humanise their work and to appropriately moderate levels of intimacy between worker and client.

Optimism

If the worker believes the client can change and if the client believes the worker can help it seems, from evidence in general counselling settings, that outcomes will be better.

Martin Seligman reviewed some of the research in this area in his books *Learned Optimism* (1990) and *The Optimistic Child* (1995). He reported on a particular study conducted in a school in the United States which offered a program in optimistic thinking to depressed children. The children subsequently demonstrated long-term reductions in depression. Seligman (1995) also cited a number of studies which have used the notion of learned optimism to facilitate cognitive change and behaviour change in aggressive and violent boys.

Work by Bandura and his colleagues (1977) has pointed to the importance of self-efficacy in general counselling situations: in other words the belief people have that they will be able to perform or cope with new behaviours and achieve their goals. Most of Bandura's work is done with voluntary clients with a focus on phobias; nonetheless, the principles seem to have more general applicability. Anne-Linda Furstenberg and Kathleen Rounds (1995), for example, discuss the applicability of self-efficacy to social work settings.

A study by Stuart Kirk and Gary Koeske (1995) in mental health found that newly hired case managers recruited to work with difficult mental health clients did better if they were 'optimistic' rather than 'realistic'. Case managers (direct practice workers) who had higher expectations and hopefulness generally than other colleagues enjoyed higher levels of job satisfaction and were less likely to quit their positions. The study unfortunately did not examine client outcomes although an earlier study by Gottschalk (1973) found a relationship between levels of hope among clients in a mental health clinic and subsequent improvement in the clients' mental health.

It does appear that an optimistic approach may be an important factor in effective work in welfare settings. This concept is perhaps particularly important in work with involuntary clients where there seems to be a tendency toward pessimism. Mary Russell (1990) refers to a number of studies in mental health and child protection settings which suggest that workers tend to be pessimistic about the likelihood of clients' improvement. She refers to a study with intellectually disabled clients in which workers underestimated the goals and daily activities of clients, and to a study with child protection workers who were pessimistic about the likelihood of preventing abuse and changing clients' behaviour.

The concepts of hope, self-efficacy and optimism run through much of the helping literature. Pro-social modelling and reinforcement with their focus on positives, and problem solving with its focus on modest goals and short-term successes, are consistent with these concepts. Similarly ego psychology (Goldstein 1995), solution-focused therapy (DeJong & Miller 1996) and other strengths-based approaches (e.g. Scott & O'Neill 1996) focus on positives and a belief on the part of the worker that clients can change.

On the other hand, the pro-social approach would suggest that worker optimism about the client's capacity to change needs to be balanced with a willingness by the worker to challenge pro-criminal or anti-social comments and actions. Nonetheless optimism does appear to be an important factor in effective work with involuntary clients.

Self-disclosure

In workshops I have conducted for probation officers and child protection workers, participants have expressed very different views about the issue of self-disclosure. Some workers feel that any level of self-disclosure is inappropriate. Participants suggest that they are often asked questions like: 'How old are you?' or 'Do you have children?'. Some respond that it is not the client's business. Others believe that giving some personal information about their own family and interests enhances the working relationship.

Again there is not a lot of research on this subject in relation to involuntary clients. Researching this area is difficult because self-disclosure seems to be so dependent on the particular context of interviews. Dean Hepworth and his colleagues (1997), in a brief review of social work literature on self-disclosure, suggest that the results are so mixed that little can be concluded from them.

However a number of studies in work with involuntary clients suggest that some level of self-disclosure may be helpful. Shulman's (1991) study in child protection found that self-disclosure, along with sharing worker's feelings, was positively related to client perceptions of worker helpfulness and client outcomes.

Shulman refers to the specific example of responding to the questions: 'How old are you and do you have children?' and he suggests that rather than dismissing the client in this situation the question can be used to explore the roles of the worker and the client. Shulman argues that the question should be answered honestly and be followed by an exploration of the client's apprehensions about the worker's ability to understand what it is like for the client.

The concept of presenting as a pro-social model to clients also involves some level of self-disclosure. Andrews and Bonta (1994:204) refer to comments such as 'I had a similar problem at your age' as being consistent with a pro-social approach. Similarly workers were encouraged in my study (Trotter 1993) to use some self-disclosure. A study by Alexander et al. (1978) of family therapy for young offenders also found that self-disclosure by therapists (among other relationship factors) was related to lower reoffending by clients.

On the other hand, Hepworth et al. (1997) considered two studies which reported increased symptomatic behaviour in paranoid schizophrenics following personal self-disclosure by practitioners.

The extent to which self-disclosure is appropriate in work with involuntary clients is therefore uncertain. It seems to be heavily dependent on the particular context in which the work takes place. I raise it here because it is an issue which is frequently spoken about by both students and professional workers and because it does appear to be a factor which may be related to client outcomes and worker effectiveness. Like the use of humour, it seems that workers with involuntary clients should not be afraid to make some use of self-disclosure in appropriate situations.

The issue of self-disclosure, along with the other relationship factors, is discussed further in Chapter 6.

Case planning, case management and the use of community resources

Involuntary clients in many cases are involved with a range of agencies and workers. For example, a family involved in child protection could be simultaneously working with a family support worker, a drug treatment worker, a domestic violence counsellor, a school welfare worker, a child psychologist, a probation officer, a housing worker, a financial counsellor and district nursing staff.

In the 1960s and 1970s in many countries around the world there was a move toward integrating welfare services so that families would receive a generic service from one, or at most a few workers. In more recent times, however, specialisation has flourished and the situation described above, where one client family could find itself interacting with as many as ten direct practice workers, is not uncommon.

Effective practice in these situations involves coordinated case planning and case management. Rubin (1985), in his review of the effectiveness of social work practice, comments that a common thread in effective programs with physically and mentally disabled clients was support for case management principles. Case managers followed up referrals, did case plans, made links with community resources and facilitated consistency in treatment.

Anne Fortune (1992) considers the role of case management in the context of inadequate resources and emphasises the advantages for clients of a coordinated approach. She points to a number of studies which suggest that casework outcomes are improved, for both voluntary and involuntary clients, when direct practice workers go beyond their 'comfortable' referral networks and when they have an understanding of bureaucratic procedures.

The potential of welfare services to be harmful as well as helpful, and the increasing specialisation of welfare services, points to the need for direct practice workers to coordinate the services which are offered to clients. Where this does not occur the effective work done by one direct practice worker could well be undone by another. An approach to case management which monitors the work done by other agencies and which involves them in planning as suggested by Jack Rothman (1991) is likely to be more successful.

I have argued in this chapter that effective work with involuntary clients involves the worker utilising the key skills of role clarification, a pro-social approach and problem solving. In situations where several workers are involved, the roles of those workers inevitably become harder to define and the consistent application of these skills is likely to be more difficult.

The extent to which case management skills can deal with this problem is doubtful. There is little research which can tell us about the relative advantages of specialised and generic services. It is apparent, however, that if numerous workers are involved with a client it will be more difficult to ensure that key components of effective casework services are present. Given the generic nature of the key skills for work with involuntary clients, outcomes might be improved by maximising continuity of service with individual workers rather than referral to specialised services.

Nonetheless workers must work within systems which often involve a proliferation of specialised agencies and services. The best method of enhancing outcomes for clients in this situation seems to be a rigorous approach to case management. This issue is discussed further in Chapter 5.

Work with families

There is a body of research which suggests that work with families can be effective in changing the behaviour of involuntary clients and in improving family functioning. This appears to be particularly so if the work with families is based on the principles of effective practice discussed in this chapter.

Alexander and Parsons (1973) undertook a study with young offenders which aimed to examine the effectiveness of different forms of family intervention. Whilst this study was done more than two decades ago, it provides an excellent illustration of the potential for work with involuntary clients to be both positive and negative. The study was undertaken with a group of minor 'delinquents'. These young people (aged thirteen to sixteen) had been arrested or detained by a juvenile court for offences such as running away, truanting, shoplifting, or possession of soft drugs. Families were randomly assigned to one of four treatment conditions.

One of the treatment conditions included a short-term behavioural family intervention program using modelling and re-inforcement by therapists of clear family communication patterns, clear presentation of demands, and alternative solutions and nego-tiation of privileges. Use was also made of contingency contracting involving an exchange of tasks or favours between family members: in other words, an approach incorporating the principles of problem solving and pro-social modelling and reinforcement.

The study compared three control groups to the treatment group: a client-centred family group, which focused on client and family feelings; a psychodynamic group sponsored by the Mormon Church with a focus on insight; and a group which received no treatment.

Reoffence rates after six to eighteen months were 50 per cent in the no treatment group; 47 per cent in the client-centred group; 73 per cent in the psychodynamic group; and 26 per cent in the short-term family behavioural treatment group.

In other words, the group which used an approach consistent with the principles of effective practice with involuntary clients had a reoffence rate of about half that of the control groups, even lower in comparison with the psychodynamic control group. Subsequent studies using the same approach (now referred to as functional family therapy), in some instances with more serious young offenders, have found similar positive results with sizeable reductions in reoffending rates (Alexander et al. 1978; Barton et al. 1985; Gordon et al. 1988; Gordon & Arbuthnot 1990).

Gerald Patterson and his colleagues at the Social Learning Center in Oregon have also reported positive outcomes in a number of studies of parent-training programs in which parents are taught behavioural methods of modifying their children's behaviour (Forgatch & Patterson 1989). Andrews and Bonta (1994) cited an unpublished study undertaken by the Oregon group with juvenile offenders which reported a reduced level of delinquent activity by participants (Marlowe et al. 1989).

Work in mental health has also pointed to the advantages of involving family. Mary Russell (1990) reviewed effective practices in work with mental health patients and pointed to a number of studies which found lower rates of relapse where family members were offered education about the nature of the client's illness with a view to coping with client symptoms. Again she referred to the effectiveness of psycho-educational programs as opposed to psychodynamic ones.

Neil DeChillo (1993) examined collaboration between social workers and families of patients with severe mental illness. He found that higher levels of collaboration were significantly correlated with satisfaction with social work services. Lynn Videka Sherman (1988), in her meta-analysis of intervention methods with chronic mental health patients, describes a home-visit based family intervention based on social learning theory and family education which resulted in a threefold reduction in hospitalisations for schizophrenic patients.

Positive outcomes have also been reported in relation to involving family in treatment of drug and alcohol abuse. Barry Loneck (1995) points to the vital role that family members can play in encouraging people with alcohol and drug problems to accept treatment, particularly when those people are resistant to receiving help.

William Reid (1985), in his book on family problem solving, reviews the evidence in support of this approach. He points to studies with parents and their children in family welfare settings and work with families in psychiatric settings which have led to positive outcomes. In a subsequent publication Reid (1992) refers to five studies which have successfully used parent training, often including anger control procedures, with parents at risk for child abuse or neglect. He suggests that these programs have produced better outcomes with such parents than alternative programs.

My own work (Trotter 1997c) examining the effectiveness of family problem-solving approaches with a range of voluntary and involuntary clients also suggests that the use of this approach with family groups is effective. My study involved teaching the basics of the family problem-solving model (as outlined in Chapter 7) to a group of final-year social work students and also to a group of professional welfare workers. The students and the workers then made use of the model with eighteen client families in local welfare agencies in Melbourne, Australia. For the most part these clients were either involuntary or partially voluntary. Clients, workers and students were then followed up after the completion of an average of eight counselling sessions.

Ninety-five per cent of the workers and students who participated in the study stated that they found the intervention to be successful. Ninety per cent of the clients indicated that their primary problem had improved by the end of treatment. And 100 per cent of the clients indicated that they benefited from the intervention.

This study did not involve control groups or long-term follow-up, however it at least indicates that family problem-solving skills can be learned relatively quickly and that workers and clients find the family problem-solving process helpful. It is consistent with the research evidence that for many involuntary clients, work with families, particularly of an educational or problem-solving nature, may be a preferable method of work.

Short-term versus long-term intervention

Reid and Shyne (1969) nearly three decades ago published a study which compared long- and short-term treatment in a child welfare setting. They concluded that, in terms of client satisfaction with service, short-term treatment was preferable. Ray Thomlinson (1984), in his review of effective casework practices, suggests that structured time-limited intervention is at least as effective as less structured open-ended intervention. Similar findings were seen in Videka Sherman's (1988) meta-analysis with mentally ill clients.

William Reid (1997b), in a review of time-limited services, points to studies supporting the value of such services with adult probationers, the chronically mentally ill, and parents seeking reunification with children in foster care. He also points to several studies which suggest the value of specific extensions of service rather than open-ended treatment.

In contrast with this, Jones and Alcabes (1993) point to a number of research studies which suggest that the most potent factor in positive outcomes in work with drug-addicted clients is the length of time in treatment. The longer they stayed in treatment the better they did.

To some extent, therefore, the evidence is equivocal in relation to time-limited work. In any case, involuntary clients are often on court orders for a specific period of time and work needs to be long term. In these instances it may be appropriate to make use of structured approaches which pursue time-limited goals within the period of intervention. In situations where short-term work is an option it seems to be as effective as long-term work with most client groups.

Client factors

This book focuses on worker practices and characteristics and how they relate to client outcomes in work with involuntary clients. It was pointed out earlier, however, that there are a number of other factors which also influence client outcomes. Some of these can be controlled or at least influenced by the direct practice worker. Two of these include the level of risk of a client and peer group influence. The issue of client motivation and its relationship to outcomes is also discussed in this section.

Focus on high-risk clients
The meta-analysis by Don Andrews and his colleagues (1990) points to the importance of workers focusing on high-risk rather than

low-risk clients in work with adult offenders. High-risk clients are those who are assessed as likely to reoffend whereas low-risk clients are assessed as unlikely to reoffend. It is argued that whilst high-risk offenders are likely to benefit from casework services, low-risk offenders may in fact be stigmatised by those services and become more criminal. (This notion is known as the 'risk principle'.)

One particular study by Andrews et al. (1986) found that high-risk probationers who received intensive supervision from volunteers reoffended at about half the rate of other offenders. In contrast, low-risk probationers who received intensive supervision offended at twice the expected rate. Similar outcomes were found in a study with juvenile offenders (Fo & O'Donnell 1974). A study with parolees also found lower offence rates among high-risk offenders who received supervision but not among low-risk offenders who received supervision (Lunden 1989).

The use of risk prediction profiles which categorise risk levels of offenders is common in corrections settings, and the appropriate use of such profiles does seem to relate to improved outcomes for offenders. The reader is referred to Andrews and Bonta (1994) for an example of a risk prediction profile for adult offenders.

Risk prediction frameworks and profiles are also commonly used in child protection settings (e.g. Orton & Rich 1988). In most instances these assessments are used to help make decisions about levels of service which are to be offered to clients and to help make decisions about placement of children. A review of research relating to risk prediction in child protection by Peter Lyons et al. (1996) suggests that it is widespread in child protection although the frameworks used tend to be developed through consensus between workers rather than an empirical process.

Similarly, risk prediction is sometimes used in mental health settings, although again the risk prediction processes are often based on clinical rather than empirical measures (Murdach 1996).

At this stage the research seems to be insufficient to say that the risk principle which applies in corrections also applies in child protection or in work with other groups of involuntary clients. It could be, however, that research in this area would lead to similar findings to those in corrections.

It does appear that there are real advantages in focusing on those clients who are most in need of service. There is some evidence that use of empirically developed risk assessment profiles and frameworks which predict the likelihood of further offending or anti-social behaviour can assist in this process in corrections, child protection and with other groups of involuntary clients (Andrews & Bonta 1994; Andrews et al. 1990; Bergman et al. 1993; Lyons 1996; Waterson & Carnie 1992).

Peer group association
In work with involuntary clients, association with an anti-social peer group can be a factor which leads to poorer outcomes. The impact of an anti-social peer group can be seen in the client's day-to-day environment or it can occur within an intervention program.

In my study in corrections (Trotter 1995b), I examined the relationship between reoffending rates of probationers and the nature of their community work placements. (Probationers in many instances were required to undertake community work. This involved working either alone or with groups of offenders on non-profit projects of some sort, for example, gardening or maintenance at schools, or assisting in tasks at a sheltered workshop for the intellectually disabled.)

It was evident that offenders who were placed on community worksites with groups of other offenders were significantly more likely to reoffend. In fact for offenders under the age of 21 the chance of them going to prison during the period of probation was three times greater if they were placed on a group worksite as opposed to an individual worksite. The differences could not be explained by the risk levels of the probationers. The magnitude of these differences is surprising, however similar results were found in a study conducted by Gil McIvor (1992) in Scotland. Ronald Akers (1994) suggests that:

> Other than one's prior deviant behaviour the best single predictor of the onset, continuance or desistance of crime and delinquency is differential association with conforming or law violating peers . . . Virtually every study that includes a peer association variable finds it to be significantly and, usually, most strongly related to delinquency, alcohol and drug abuse, adult crime and other forms of deviant behaviour. (Akers 1994:104)

Colin Roberts (1993) argues, in a review of effective corrections programs, that the high reoffending rates of institutionalised offenders may be explained, at least in part, by the criminal subculture of prisons and the reinforcement of criminal attitudes.

The impact of peer group association with other groups of involuntary clients is less clear cut, although Lynn Videka Sherman, in her meta-analysis of the effectiveness of interventions in mental health, found that 'between-session contacts among clients participating in group treatment' was related to poorer outcomes for clients (1988:328).

Groupwork

This is not to say that there are not successful programs with involuntary clients. There is, for example, research support for the effectiveness of group counselling for violent men (e.g. Mullender 1996), for drug users (e.g. Milgram & Rubin 1992), for psychiatric clients (e.g. Videka Sherman 1988) and for offenders (e.g. Ferguson 1983; Raynor & Vanstone 1996).

The focus of this book is clearly on direct practice with individuals and families rather than group work, and the arguments for and against the use of groups are complex (e.g. Moore et al. 1997; Reid 1997b). The research does suggest, however, that effective group work is likely to be characterised by similar practices to those referred to in this chapter. For example, Joan Ferguson (1982) in her meta-analysis of group work with offenders, found that groups were successful when they included pro-social modelling and reinforcement, problem solving and an advocacy broker facility. In another example Edleson and Syers (1990) found that short-term (twelve sessions) educationally focused groups for perpetrators of domestic violence were more effective in reducing the incidence of violence (as reported by partners) compared with longer-term (32 sessions) unstructured, self-help groups.

It does appear that whilst group work is often effective, the general mixing of involuntary clients has the potential to be problematic. The anti-social attitudes and actions which have led clients into the system may well be reinforced by programs which encourage association between people who have similar views, particularly if this association is not part of a program which makes use of effective practice principles.

Motivation

One factor which is often raised by students and professional workers relates to client levels of motivation. Students and professional workers often comment that you cannot change someone who does not want to change, that workers' energies may be wasted on unmotivated clients. Yet the issue is more complex than this.

Involuntary clients are for the most part motivated by a court order or the threat of some legal action. Given a choice they would not be involved with the direct practice worker. Nonetheless once they are involved in the client–worker relationship they may be motivated to different degrees. That motivation is, however, very hard to measure. A perpetrator of domestic violence might, for example, say that he wishes to change his violent behaviour toward his wife, or a drug user might say that he wishes to give up drugs. The behaviour of these clients, on the other hand, may not reflect this.

The complexity of the motivation issue is highlighted by studies in probation supervision which suggest that high-risk offenders, perhaps the ones least likely to be motivated to change, are most likely to benefit from supervision (Andrews et al. 1990). Lynn Videka Sherman (1988) found no association between voluntary and involuntary participation and outcomes among mental health clients. Another study found that people with alcohol and drug problems who were resistant to treatment could be encouraged to become involved by confrontation and encouragement from family members (Loneck 1995).

In contrast Jones and Alcabes (1993) argue that in child protection readiness to change is important in terms of improved client outcomes. A study by Thomas O'Hare (1996) in mental health also supports this view. O'Hare considered 'readiness to change' in court-ordered and voluntary clients in mental health. He made use of a stages-of-change-scale involving four stages: pre-contemplation, contemplation, action and maintenance. He found that voluntary clients were much more likely to express engagement in the change process, although many involuntary clients were also interested in changing. He suggests that 28 per cent of involuntary clients were at least at the contemplation stage, compared with 55 per cent of voluntary clients.

The issue of client motivation is therefore a complex one. Levels of client motivation may be very difficult to separate from the interaction which exists between worker and client. Perhaps the most important point in relation to client motivation is made by Beulah Compton and Burt Galaway (1994) when they say that you cannot expect a client to be motivated to work toward goals which they have had no part in developing. Certainly the notion that involuntary clients are unmotivated and therefore cannot change is an oversimplification.

APPROACHES THAT DON'T WORK

Whilst the research strongly suggests that some approaches to work with involuntary clients are indeed, effective, it is apparent, however, that direct practice with involuntary clients has the capacity to be both helpful and harmful. Approaches which blame, punish and judge clients in the hope that their behaviour will change seem doomed to failure—whether they are used with young offenders, parents who have abused their children, perpetrators of domestic violence or any other involuntary clients. This is not to say that there are not often occasions when the inevitable consequences of clients' actions need to be pointed out to them, or that pro-criminal or anti-social actions and comments should not be challenged. I argue strongly in Chapter 4 that they should be. However blaming and punishment, particularly where they are not accompanied by attempts to address client problems or to reinforce positives, do not work. The poor success of day-in-gaol programs (in which young offenders are placed in gaol for a day) and similar programs which have attempted to scare young offenders into going straight provides a good example of this (Lipsey 1991; Gendreau 1996). Similarly, child protection programs have found that the threat of imprisonment or removing children is not necessarily effective in changing parental behaviour (Gough 1993). Lambert et al. (1986) refer to therapist's aggressive tactics being related to deteriorating outcomes.

Interventions which focus on insight alone or the relationship alone and do not include problem solving or pro-social dimensions have limited support in work with involuntary clients (Andrews et al. 1990; Gough 1993).

Interventions which focus on worker goals rather than achievable client goals or goals agreed on between worker and client do not seem to work (Thomlinson 1984; Rubin 1985; Jones & Alcabes 1993).

Poor outcomes have been achieved in situations where there is uncertainty by the client or the worker about the purpose of the intervention, about the role of the worker as social controller or helper, and about how authority should be used (Andrews et al. 1979; Videka Sherman 1988; Shulman 1991; Jones & Alcabes 1993).

A pessimistic view about the client's capacity to change, a focus on what clients are doing wrong, and a reluctance to encourage and reward positive behaviours are all related to poorer outcomes for involuntary clients (Andrews et al. 1979; Masters et al. 1987; Shulman 1991; Trotter 1996a).

A focus on the individual and viewing the individual as the problem rather than focusing on the client in the family and social context also seems to be related to poorer outcomes for involuntary clients (Rubin 1985; Fortune 1992).

AN EMPIRICAL PRACTICE MODEL

The following chapters of this book outline a practice model based on the research about what works and on the model which was used in my own work in corrections (Trotter 1996a). It focuses particularly on role clarification, a pro-social approach and collaborative problem solving. Problem solving with family groups is also discussed.

Other practice principles which the research suggests are related to effective work with involuntary clients are incorporated into the practice model either directly or through the use of case examples. In particular the model incorporates the use of self-disclosure, confrontation and humour, time limits, case management principles and the use of community resources. Whilst this book presents an empirical practice model, reference is also made to other sources of knowledge referred to in Chapter 1, such as values and organisational expectations.

The book attempts therefore to incorporate a range of skills and approaches into an integrated practice model. There is some evidence from meta-analytic reviews that multi-component approaches such as this are more effective (Andrews et al. 1990; Reid 1997a). In other words, more effective approaches involve the use of a number of different approaches rather than relying on one single theory such as behaviourist theory or psychoanalytic theory.

It will have become clear that much of my own work on the development of this practice model has been in a correctional setting. I have argued, however, that the principles underlying the model apply generally in work with involuntary clients. This is increasingly evident from work I am currently doing on further development of the model in child protection (Trotter 1997c) and in work I have done in family welfare settings (Trotter 1997b).

Empirical practice and theory and other practice models

I suggested in Chapter 1 that theories help to guide research and explain research findings. One would expect, therefore, an effective practice model to be both supported by research findings and consistent with one or more theoretical perspectives. In other words, a practice model should not only work, it should be clear why it works.

It is not the aim in this book to examine casework theories in any detail. The practice model presented is derived primarily from research findings. Nonetheless some brief discussion about the relationship between this practice model and some of the more popular casework theories and alternative practice models is appropriate.

Ecological systems theory
Systems theory points to the interrelatedness of people and different events. The term 'ecological systems theory' uses a biological metaphor to illustrate the sometimes dramatic impact that intervening in one system may have on other systems.

Ecological systems theory points to the sometimes unexpected impacts that casework interventions might have. For example, a worker might facilitate reading classes for a mature-aged illiterate client. The newly acquired reading skill might impact on a spouse who feels less needed. This might in turn threaten a marital relationship, which has been sustained by dependency. This might then impact on the client's relationships with her children who become involved somehow in the failing relationship. This might then impact on grandchildren, who are close to the grandparents, and so on.

Systems theory also recognises the importance of roles which are ascribed to individuals and groups, for example, roles as parents or children, as women or men, or as worker or client. Systems theory highlights the importance of being aware of roles in work with clients.

Systems theory underlies the practice model presented in this book. The practice model highlights the importance of understanding the client's situation in terms of the wider environment. It also highlights the importance of clarity about role and the difficulties caseworkers may experience when they, or their clients, are confused about role expectations.

The reader is referred to Germain and Gitterman (1996) for a recent publication which describes in detail a systems approach to direct welfare practice.

Behaviour theory and cognitive behavioural treatments
Behaviour theory suggests, among other things, that anti-social behaviour may be developed as a result of association with anti-social peers, by exposure to anti-social role models and by reinforcement and rewarding of anti-social behaviour. On the other hand, pro-social behaviour may be developed through association with pro-social peer groups, exposure to pro-social role models and reinforcing and rewarding pro-social behaviour (Hudson & McDonald 1986; Ackers 1994).

Behaviour theory is therefore central to, and provides an explanation for, the positive research findings associated with the pro-social approach. Behaviour theory is discussed further in Chapter 4.

Cognitive theory, unlike behaviour theory, recognises that learning processes are influenced by thoughts and feelings. Cognitive therapy, rather than concentrating on behaviours, focuses on thought patterns and changing distorted thinking (Hepworth et al. 1997). Whilst the pro-social approach is primarily behaviourist, problem solving, role clarification and relationship skills focus on cognitive change as well as behaviour change. The practice model, as it is presented in this book, encourages clients to change anti-social thinking as well as anti-social behaviours. It therefore has something in common with cognitive therapies.

For more detail on cognitive behavioural approaches the reader is referred to Masters et al. (1987).

Feminist casework
Whilst there are a number of different feminist approaches, Jan Fook (1993) suggests that there are some common themes in a feminist approach to casework. In particular feminist casework focuses on the way in which patriarchal systems disadvantage women through sex role stereotyping and devaluing of women's experience. Feminist approaches to casework highlight the importance of helping women to understand their situation from a gender perspective (Fook 1993).

In an earlier publication (1986), Fook summarises the differences between feminist therapy and traditional therapy as incorporating a 'more equal relationship formed with the client, an emphasis on feminist interpretations of social expectations and personal identity and the focus on personal strength and change, rather than pathology and adjustment' (Fook 1986:55).

Fook suggests a number of strategies and techniques which are relevant to feminist casework. These include more equal interviewing settings (e.g. in the client's home); gathering of information in the assessment stage which relates to gender role expectations and labelling; the use of therapeutic techniques such as empathy and critical questioning to identify socially conditioned assumptions; the use of equal and non-authoritarian relationship styles; and providing information and advocating on behalf of the client. Fook (1986, 1993) also refers to the value of modelling as an educational process.

The practice model presented in this book has elements in common with feminist casework as it is described by Fook (1987). For example, its focus, like that of feminist casework, is on equal relationships and on positives and strengths rather than on negatives or client shortcomings.

The pro-social approach, in recognising the importance of values in the direct practice process, also provides a framework for the practical implementation of a feminist approach. The worker can identify and reinforce comments and actions which recognise feminist interpretations of events. The worker can model behaviour which is consistent with feminist values. Through the problem-solving process the worker can also encourage clients to explore feminist interpretations of problems.

I would argue, like Andre Ivanoff, Elizabeth Robinson and Betty Blythe (1987:419), that 'an ethical commitment to employ those interventions most likely to solve client's problems' is very consistent with a feminist approach to casework. Later chapters include some case examples which illustrate how the practice model described in this book can facilitate feminist casework.

Radical casework
Radical casework has much in common with feminist casework. It is based on a premise that client problems derive largely from socio-economic or structural factors such as class and role expectations, inequality, poverty, poor housing, unemployment, inadequate social security systems and so on. Radical approaches to casework focus on helping clients to become aware of their situation from a socio-political perspective and not to accept blame for their disadvantage. Clients may be encouraged to become involved in social action which aims to change social structures. Similarly workers might be involved in social action in addition to

advocating for their clients. For more detail on this subject the reader is referred again to Jan Fook's (1993) book *Radical Casework*.

Radical casework has particular relevance for workers with involuntary clients who often work for bureaucracies which may play a part in perpetuating disadvantage. The intervention model presented in this book is to some extent consistent with radical casework. Whilst it focuses on direct practice rather than social change processes, it does aim to be non blaming, to define problems from the client's rather than the worker's or the organisation's perspective and to address client issues in a broad context. It is particularly concerned about the inappropriate imposition of worker and organisational values. This subject is discussed further in Chapters 4 and 5.

Task-centred casework

William Reid and his colleagues began developing task-centred casework more than two decades ago (Reid & Epstein 1972) and a lot has been written about it since this time (e.g. Doel & Marsh 1992; Reid 1992). Task-centred casework is a problem-solving model for work with both voluntary and involuntary clients. It focuses particularly on the development of tasks to address problems.

Task-centred casework has many similarities with the practice model presented in this book. In particular the problem-solving and the family problem-solving chapters owe much to the work of William Reid. This book does, however, adapt the task-centred model particularly to work with involuntary clients. The model presented here also, unlike task-centred approaches, focuses particularly on role clarification and the pro-social approach.

Solution-focused approaches

Solution-focused approaches (e.g. DeShazer 1988) are popular in some areas of work with involuntary clients. Solution-focused work involves focusing on client strengths and focusing on solutions rather than problems. It involves examining what clients want to be different in their lives (their goals), and what resources they can make use of in achieving their goals. It involves exploring for exceptions or identifying times when the problems were not present.

Again the practice model presented here has some things in common with these approaches. In particular, like solution-focused approaches, it highlights the importance of optimism and of identifying and reinforcing positives and client strengths. It also focuses on developing goals and tasks or solutions. The model presented in this book is, however, unlike solution-focused approaches in its focus on research findings, its focus on identifying and exploring problems, and its specific promotion of pro-social actions and expressions.

Other approaches
There are, of course, myriad different theories and models which influence direct practice with involuntary clients. I have attempted here simply to highlight a few of the similarities and differences between the empirical model presented in this book and some of the more popular theories and models which are often used in work with involuntary clients.

SUMMARY

The research on work with involuntary clients suggests that some things work better than others. There are certain generic practice principles which seem to be effective with most if not all groups of involuntary clients. These include: accurate role clarification; working with problems and goals as they are defined by the client; and modelling and reinforcing pro-social values.

There are a number of other approaches or practice skills which seem to relate to positive outcomes, however in some instances the research is equivocal about them and in other instances they seem to be effective with only some groups of involuntary clients. These include: the client–worker (or casework) relationship; case planning, case management and the use of community resources; work with families; and short-term interventions. There are also a number of client factors which relate to outcomes such as risk levels, peer group association and client motivation.

There are some approaches which the research suggests are generally related to minimal impact or poorer outcomes. These include: approaches which seek merely to blame or punish clients; approaches which focus exclusively on insight or the client–worker relationship; working with problems and goals defined by the worker alone; confusion and dishonesty on the part of the worker about role and how authority will be used; pessimism and negative focus; and failing to see the client in a family and social context.

A practice model for work with involuntary clients has been presented here and some comments made about how this model relates to other theories and models. The following chapters outline the practice model in more detail.

3 | Role clarification

WHAT ARE WE here for? What are we hoping to get out of this? What do we have to do? What do we have a choice about?

The research referred to in Chapter 2 suggests that clarity about these issues on the part of worker and client is likely to be related to better outcomes for involuntary clients. The research suggests that role clarification should be viewed as one of the key skills in work with involuntary clients (Andrews et al. 1979; Videka Sherman 1988; Shulman 1991; Jones & Alcabes 1993).

Clarification of role involves workers helping their clients to understand the nature of the direct practice or casework process. It involves more than simply explaining the conditions of a court order or the mandate under which the worker operates. It is about exploring with clients the purpose of the intervention, what the worker hopes to achieve and what the client hopes to achieve.

Clarification of role is an ongoing process. It occurs at the beginning of work with involuntary clients when basic details about legal responsibilities are usually discussed. It continues throughout the intervention process as worker and client explore the purpose of their time together. An explanation of role might take a few minutes. Ongoing exploration of role and ongoing endeavours by the worker to help the client understand the role might take many hours over many interviews.

Clarification of role occurs simultaneously with other aspects of the direct practice process. A worker in any interview might be exploring with clients their perception of the role of the worker, reinforcing pro-social comments by the clients, working through the problem-solving process and making use of relationship skills such as empathy or optimism.

In seminars I have conducted with child protection workers, probation officers, school welfare workers and other workers with involuntary clients, workers have consistently referred to certain role-related issues which they believe should be discussed and explored with clients. These include: the dual (social control/welfare) role of the worker; what is negotiable and what is not negotiable and how the worker's authority might be used; the client's expectations of the worker; confidentiality and who has a right to information; the nature of the professional relationship and what this means in terms of how the worker and client interact; the role of the worker as case manager, case planner or caseworker; the client's expectations of the casework process; the expectations the worker's employing organisation places on the worker and the client; and the theoretical approach the worker takes to the work.

Clarification of role involves the worker coming to terms with these issues and helping clients to come to terms with them. The worker will often feel uncertainty about these issues and the worker's views will often change as a result of different experiences. An effective worker, however, thinks through these issues and recognises their importance in the direct practice process.

What is the nature of the role-related issues which workers might explore with involuntary clients?

DUAL ROLE: SOCIAL CONTROL AND HELPING

Chapter 1 highlighted the uncertainty workers often feel about the welfare versus social control (legalistic) dilemma. Is the primary purpose of work with involuntary clients to administer a court order and to investigate anti-social behaviour, or is it to help clients with problems? The answer to this question is rarely clear. In fact workers generally move between helping and legalistic roles at different stages of the direct practice process, even at different stages of an interview.

There are instances when workers with involuntary clients adopt a strongly legalistic focus. For example, a worker might be interviewing a father who has abused his child with a view to removing the child if he appears to be in danger of being injured again. The worker must collect detailed information about the circumstances of the father and the child to make an assessment of the child's immediate safety.

The worker may feel in this situation that it is misleading to the client to suggest that she has a helping or problem-solving role. For example, the child protection worker by working through issues or problems could lead the client to divulge information which could lead to the subsequent removal of the child. The worker might feel that the use of a welfare or problem-solving approach could give the client a sense of having been misled or trapped.

In other instances the worker might adopt a less legalistic and more welfare-oriented or problem-solving approach. In these instances the more legalistic aspects of the work may be difficult. A child protection worker, after a number of visits, may feel that she is progressing well with a mother who has neglected her child. The worker may have worked through a number of problems and developed a close working relationship with the mother and her child, even though there continue to be serious concerns about the mother's parenting practices. The worker might feel in this instance that discussion about legalistic issues (e.g. the possible need for a return to court) would interfere with the working relationship.

This dilemma exists across the range of involuntary clients. For example, a homeless youth might be befriended by an outreach youth worker. The youth worker might be concerned about the young person's excessive drug use and feel it is necessary to report the matter to the police or child protection authorities. The youth worker might focus immediately on her legalistic role and feel that discussing her role as a helper in these circumstances is misleading. On the other hand, in other situations the youth worker might feel pressured to focus exclusively on the helping role because she fears many young people would have nothing to do with her if they thought their disclosures might be reported to police or other authorities.

These dilemmas are real ones for direct practice workers. The intervention model which is presented in this book, however, favours an approach which strikes a balance between the social control and welfare functions. There is some research evidence which suggests that an approach which achieves this balance is likely to be of most benefit to involuntary clients. For example, I recently undertook a review of new books on community corrections programs around the world (Trotter 1996b). These books suggest that many probation programs focus on welfare or punishment rather than a combination of the two. The books point to the importance of a balanced approach if programs are to be successful.

Similarly, in child protection work, getting the balance right between welfare and social control is important. Lawrence Shulman (1991) found that effective child protection workers focused on and emphasised the dual nature of their role in discussions with clients.

There will always be occasions in work with involuntary clients when either the welfare or legalistic aspects of the worker's role predominate for a part of or even for the duration of work with a particular client. However, even in situations where the focus of the work is on legalistic issues, such as the first child protection visit, it is important that the client understands that the worker also has a helping role. The early child protection interviews can begin to prepare clients for the problem-solving process which may follow.

Lawrence Shulman, in his book on child protection in Canada, gives an example of the type of comments about the dual role which might be made by a worker on an initial visit: 'I am here because we received a call from someone who felt you might be neglecting your child. I have to investigate such calls to see if there is any truth in them. I also want to see if there is any way we might be helpful to you' (Shulman 1991:27).

The worker might then go on to discuss with the client how she can help and what 'to investigate' actually means.

Similar comments can be made with other involuntary clients. For example, a probation officer might comment: 'My job involves making sure you carry out the conditions of the court order. It is also an equally important part of my work to help you with any problems which might have caused you to be put on probation.'

To sum up: workers with involuntary clients should recognise the difficulties inherent in their dual role as social controllers and helpers and they should help their clients to understand the nature of this dual role. Frequent and regular discussion with clients about this issue, along with the other role-related issues addressed below, is likely to lead to improved outcomes for clients.

WHAT IS NEGOTIABLE AND WHAT IS NOT

In helping clients to understand the nature of the dual role of the worker, the worker and client will often discuss negotiable and non-negotiable aspects of the intervention. Involuntary clients should be clear about what is required of them and what are the likely consequences if they do not comply with those requirements. They should be clear about whether these are legal requirements, organisational requirements or worker requirements.

For example, a child protection worker working with a family on a court order may have power to remove a child in certain circumstances. In what circumstances might this happen? Would a further incidence of physical assault automatically result in this occurring? Are there other 'bottom lines' with which the parent must comply to keep the child? Can the parents use other forms of discipline with the child? For example, is any smacking acceptable?

Similar questions can be asked in relation to probation. A probationer is required to report to his probation officer on a regular basis. What happens if the probationer fails to report? What if he misses one, two or three appointments? What if he has a good reason for being unable to attend? When the probationer does report what is then required of him? Is involvement in a problem-solving process with the worker voluntary or involuntary? What if the probationer chooses to attend as required but only gives basic information and refuses to discuss personal issues? In other words, does the client have a right to refuse treatment? What if the probationer wishes to go on holidays? Can he make up appointments by doing two in one week rather than one each week?

These issues also arise in settings where clients might be considered more voluntary. For example, a school welfare worker or school counsellor might be asked to work with a student displaying behavioural problems in class following the separation of his parents. Does the student have to see the counsellor? What will happen if he fails to do so? What will be the consequences if the student sees the counsellor but refuses to discuss issues with her? Does the student have a right to stop the counsellor talking to the student's parents?

Lloyd Owen and Denbigh Richards (1995) consider negotiable and non-negotiable areas from a slightly different perspective in terms of legally or voluntarily derived mandates for intervention. They point out that it is important that the client understands whether non-negotiable requirements are based on a legal mandate, an organisational expectation or simply a worker's expectation. For example, a probation officer might have a legal mandate to require a probationer to report regularly, however, she might have an organisational mandate to work with the client on issues which relate to the offending behaviour. Failure to work on drug-related issues, for example, might not in this instance lead to a return of the matter to court but it might lead to increased frequency of appointments imposed by the probation service.

Work with involuntary clients involves being clear about negotiable and non-negotiable areas and legally and non-legally derived mandates for intervention. In many instances clients may be concerned about these issues but may not be sufficiently aware or confident to articulate them. In most cases it is up to the worker to raise them and to help the client to understand them.

CONFIDENTIALITY

Confidentiality in work with involuntary clients is perhaps a misleading notion. Who can know and who cannot is a more meaningful way of talking about what happens to information passed from clients to workers.

In work with involuntary clients, information given by the client to the worker is often passed on to other places. It might, for example, be used in court reports, it might be discussed with the worker's supervisor, it might be used in case planning meetings within the worker's organisation, or it might be passed on to other agencies such as drug or psychiatric treatment agencies.

Some matters which are discussed between workers and their clients might be confidential. In other words, information about the discussion may not be passed on to anyone. For example, a mental health client might discuss with his worker his feelings of depression and worthlessness and his inability to relate to women. The worker might work through this issue with the client on the understanding that it is confidential. Or at least that any discussion about these issues with another professional would not take place without prior discussion and agreement from the client.

The issue of who can know should be discussed with clients in some detail. An open exploration of these issues is an important part of effective work with involuntary clients.

File notes

File notes may be a source of concern in work with involuntary clients. Sometimes uncertainty surrounds what access the client has to file notes. In many public welfare agencies clients and client families accumulate large files. Often they run to two or more volumes. In some instances they contain many more words than an average book. In practice situations workers sometimes bring those paper files into the interview rooms with their clients. It would be surprising if clients did not feel some curiosity or even anxiety about the material in these files.

There are instances where it may not be appropriate to allow clients to read their files, for example if they contain reports written many years earlier by professionals other than the current worker. The casual comment in a file note that a particular client was adopted or that the client's estranged father was in prison could be devastating to a young person who is unaware of these things. Care must of course be exercised in these situations.

As a general rule, however, the sharing of file notes with clients is recommended as consistent with the principles of effective practice. It is argued in Chapter 5 that sharing file notes can be used to assist in the problem-solving process.

Clients are also likely to be interested in who else can read their files. Often in work with involuntary clients, courts can subpoena files and workers can be cross-examined in relation to the content of files. Senior staff also have access to files, as do other staff members including clerical staff. In many agencies files are described as the property of the agency and access is available to most if not all agency staff.

Revelations about all the people who might have access to client files might raise anxiety in some clients. It is certainly not recommended that the worker necessarily detail all the people who might have access to a client file. Nonetheless an open approach to this issue is part of effective practice.

Discussion with clients in general terms about the limited nature of confidentiality in relation to files and other information should be a routine part of work with involuntary clients. If, for example, excerpts from a file are read to a court this should not be a surprise to the client. The worker should have discussed such a possibility at some time during the period of contact with the client.

The messages from the research discussed in Chapter 2 suggest that open, honest and frequent discussions about issues such as these are important to effective practice. Good practice with involuntary clients involves being sensitive to client concerns in these areas and discussing issues about confidentiality on a regular basis.

CASE MANAGER, CASE PLANNER OR PROBLEM SOLVER

Another issue which should be addressed with clients relates to the worker's role as case manager, case planner and problem solver. In Chapter 1 direct practice was defined as the provision of direct counselling or helping services to clients in addition to planning, oversight and referral. Case management, on the other hand, was defined more in terms of oversight and referral functions.

The worker should be clear about her particular role as a case planner, case manager or problem solver. The worker should help the client to understand the role of other workers in the helping process. The worker should explore the client's perceptions of her role and help the client to understand the different aspects of the role.

The worker should help the client to understand the specific tasks for which the worker is responsible. If the worker has a role as a case manager and case planner with much of the direct problem-solving work being done by other agencies or workers, this should be clear to the client. The worker should try to help the client understand how help will be provided for different problems, how services will be coordinated and the worker's responsibilities in this, what the client can do if services are unsatisfactory, and what happens if the client does not follow up services as planned.

It should also be clear to the client how he can participate in the case management, case planning and problem-solving processes. The client should be helped to understand his role in relation to each step of each of the processes.

CLIENT'S EXPECTATIONS

Clients may have had experience of casework services before. They may have had a number of different workers from different parts of the public welfare system. They may have developed expectations about the nature of the role of the worker. These expectations might be realistic or unrealistic. They might have derived from a culture different from that of the worker. The notion of a direct practice worker having a helping role might seem foreign to clients with particular cultural backgrounds.

An exploration of these expectations will help the worker and the client to clarify the nature of the worker's role.

There may be instances when clients make reference to previous workers. For example, a probationer might say: 'My last worker did not seem too interested in talking about my problems. All she cared about was whether I turned up for appointments.' The worker might use these comments to explore the client's expectations of the probation officer's role.

The worker might comment: 'I also believe it is absolutely essential that you turn up for appointments. However, I am concerned about other things you do. In fact, as I have explained, I hope we can work on some other issues that seem to have led to you being placed on probation. Have you ever had a probation officer who helped you with your problems?'

A probation client may be in contact with other offenders and may have developed perceptions of probation supervision from their comments. The probationer might have heard, for example, that it is possible to get away with missing every second appointment if you ring each time and make an excuse. In order to explore these issues the probation officer might ask the client what he knows about probation, how often he would expect to report, and so on. The probation officer might also ask the client if friends have been on probation and what their experiences were.

If clients have misconceptions about the nature of the worker's role, it is important that these are explored. When I started work in probation I was surprised by the number of probationers who simply failed to keep appointments and failed to notify any change of address. In due course they would be arrested and I would visit them in prison. In many cases they would say they just wanted to get away and did not realise that probation supervision could be transferred. On other occasions they had missed one appointment and thought that this would automatically result in revocation of their probation. Their misconceptions led to the cancellation of their probation and to their subsequent imprisonment.

Another example from foster care illustrates this point. A thirteen-year-old girl had been placed in numerous children's homes and foster homes. On one occasion she was abused by her foster parents. She was unable to convince her worker at the time that the placement was unsuitable and she subsequently ran away. In discussions with the new worker about what she expected from the worker she mentioned her disappointment with the previous worker. The new worker was then able to address these concerns and reassure the young person that it was part of the role of the worker to respond and follow up situations such as these. The worker was able to point out that if such a situation were to be repeated, the client should contact the worker immediately rather than simply running away. Effective work with involuntary clients involves exploring what the client expects from the intervention and clarifying misconceptions. This sometimes involves exploring the client's earlier experiences.

HELPING THE CLIENT TO UNDERSTAND THE NATURE OF THE PROFESSIONAL RELATIONSHIP

Clients and workers often have differing views about the extent to which the worker and client are friends and the extent to which the worker is an advocate for the client. A client who might comment in relation to his worker—'You are my friend and I can count on you to be on my side'—may be disappointed if the worker is forced to take action with which the client disagrees.

My study in probation (Trotter 1993) asked clients to describe the role of their supervisor. They were given a number of options to choose from including supervisor, friend, advocate, counsellor, adviser, police officer and prison officer. Forty-seven per cent described the probation officer as their friend, after supervisor (61%) and counsellor (51%). Whilst probation officers were not asked the same question it seems likely that there was a lack of congruence in relation to worker and client views about this issue. Few probation officers would describe their clients as friends.

In work with adolescents who may have few identity models, with clients experiencing depression or other mental illness, with isolated parents or victims of domestic violence, the possibility of viewing the worker as a friend is no doubt greater than in most probation situations. The potential for clients to look for more in the client–worker relationship than the worker intends is always present.

This confusion about the extent to which the worker is a friend or a professional can create particular problems with long-term and dependent clients. The issue of dependency can present as much difficulty in work with involuntary clients as issues relating to resistance. This relates in part to the fact that work with involuntary clients is often long term. Indeed, there are many instances of children being involved in the child welfare system for the bulk of their childhood and adolescence. Workers involved with families or individuals over long periods, particularly when those families and individuals lead isolated lives, have to deal regularly with the issue of dependence.

Appropriate role clarification involves the worker exploring with the client the issue of friendship and the client's expectations in this area. Before this can occur, workers of course need to be clear in their own minds about the limits of the relationship. Discussion can then take place in relation to these limits. For example, it is generally appropriate to discuss the fact that the worker is employed by an agency for a specific purpose and that the worker has a number of clients and the time she has available is limited. The worker should be clear about the extent to which she is available to talk to or visit the client between scheduled appointments.

Discussions about the nature of the direct practice process and the purpose of the intervention will also help the client to understand the limits of the relationship. The intervention process itself should involve a clear plan with specific strategies and a proposed time of termination. Even in long-term interventions the work should be broken down into stages. For example, the worker might work toward a set of goals with a drug-addicted mother over a period of three months. After the three months have elapsed a review of progress can take place and another agreement reached to work toward other goals for the next three months. This is consistent with effective practice as outlined in Chapter 2 and avoids the unstructured supportive type of worker–client relationship which may well foster client dependency.

In work with isolated clients it is important that the issue of isolation is dealt with directly. It is clearly preferable that a client develop new social networks with the help of the worker rather than the worker fulfilling these needs.

The best protection against inappropriate client dependency (and for that matter worker dependency) is the regular and frequent discussion about the role-related issues raised in this chapter and the use of a structured problem-solving approach as outlined in Chapter 5.

ORGANISATIONAL EXPECTATIONS

It can be difficult for workers to come to terms with their role in their employer organisation. In some organisations direct practice workers get clear messages from their organisations about their role. They may have opportunities to input to the organisation in relation to role-related issues. For example, staff members might regularly discuss issues with each other and senior staff relating to the welfare and social control aspects of the work. In other organisations workers may receive confused messages about their role and they may feel powerless to influence the direction of the organisation.

A working environment which helps workers to explore issues relating to their role is likely to produce workers who help clients explore issues relating to the worker's role—leading in turn to more effective work. There is support for this view in Lawrence Shulman's (1991) study in child protection, which suggests a relationship between supervisors' exploration of role with workers and workers' exploration of role with their clients.

Issues which workers might discuss with their clients include: What relationship does the worker have with the employing organisation? Does the employing organisation place restraints on the way the worker functions—for example, does the worker receive supervision and does the supervision influence decisions the worker makes?

Or does the organisation set particular policies—for example, does the organisation have a policy about the right of clients to change workers? Does the organisation require workers to complete a risk assessment profile on clients? Does the organisation have a policy about excluding men from domestic violence group coun-selling if they make threats of physical violence within the group?

Discussion about the policies of the organisation, how these impact on the worker and how they impact on work done with clients is all part of clarifying the role of the worker and client.

THEORETICAL APPROACH TO THE WORK

Many of the readers of this book, if they were to seek the services of a professional counsellor, would insist on knowing something of that person's background and theoretical approach. They might want to know what qualifications the counsellor had, the particular theoretical approach she worked from, the amount of experience she had in this type of work or whether previous clients had been helped by her.

Involuntary clients, on the whole, may not be so demanding

or articulate, nonetheless, they may have an interest in the particular approach the worker uses. Andre Ivanoff and his colleagues, in their book about involuntary clients, comment that 'the client has a right to understand the theoretical premises that guide the practitioner's choice of intervention' (Ivanoff et al. 1994:58).

In clarifying their roles workers should be open about their particular theoretical approaches and provide opportunities for clients to ask questions about them. If, for example, the worker is using a problem-solving approach it is appropriate to explain this to the client. This might involve a brief comment in a first interview but more detailed explanation in subsequent interviews.

Following training courses I have undertaken with workers with involuntary clients, some workers have displayed in their offices a list of steps relating to problem solving, role clarification and pro-social modelling and reinforcement (see Appendix). They have then worked through the various steps on the list explaining to clients the structure they are using for the intervention. This is certainly an approach I favour because it is consistent with the principle of giving clients maximum information about the case-work process and their part in it.

CASE EXAMPLES

The following examples of interviews or conversations between workers and involuntary clients illustrate an approach to the clarification of role which is consistent with the principles of effective practice. The conversations are simple and some readers may feel that 'this is what they would have done anyway', empirical practice or not. It is my belief, however, having observed many interviews conducted by experienced workers that these skills are harder to apply than they at first appear.

Whilst the interviews in this chapter and in subsequent chapters are not actual transcripts of real interviews, they have been developed in collaboration and through role plays with workers in the field.

A first interview between a child protection worker and a father who has been leaving his children unsupervised

The child protection worker in this example has received a report that the client, Jake, has on many occasions left his two children, aged five and three, at home without supervision, sometimes for several hours. The child protection worker has visited with a colleague to investigate the report. The worker is trying to help the client understand her role as a child protection worker.

Worker: Jake, I'm Janet Smith. Thank you for giving me the opportunity to come in and talk to you a little bit more about why I'm here.

Jake: OK.

Worker: As I said to you at the front door, I'm part of the child protection team at the Department of Human Services. Have you had anything to do with child protection before? Do you know what we do?

Jake: Are they the people who take children away?

Worker: That is what a lot of people think—that our job is to come and take children away. However, this happens in a very small number of cases. The vast bulk of our work is with helping families. When we receive a report that children might be at risk, then we come out to see what's happening, and to see if there's anything that the family needs that we can help them with. So there are two roles: number one is, are the children safe, and number two, what can we help the family with.

Jake: I know someone that was involved with child protection, and they didn't receive help. What they received was a lot of investigation and eventually the child was taken away for a week and then brought back again. You wouldn't believe the problems they had. And it seemed to me they'd done nothing. Has someone complained about my children?

Worker: Well, someone's raised concerns about your children, and obviously if you know someone who's had a negative experience I guess that could make you anxious to know what we're going to say and do in relation to you.

Jake: Yeah.

Worker: What we'll be doing is talking with you about what is happening, whether there's anything that is putting your children's safety at risk, and whether there's anything we can help you with. I also need to let you know that we usually work in pairs and we always take notes because there is a very small number of cases in which the matter is taken to the Children's Court and sometimes the information that we gain when we talk with families is used as part of a court report.

Jake: So this information is being written down.

Worker: Yes, we always record initial interviews.

Jake: And it can be used in court.

Worker: It can be.

Jake: Are you saying that I could have to go to court?

Worker: What I'm saying is that in a very small number of cases, perhaps 5 per cent of the total number of calls that we get, a matter might be taken to the Children's Court if we feel a child is immediately, seriously at risk of harm.

Jake: Well, my children are fine.

Worker: OK, so if your children are not immediately, seriously at risk of harm, then you wouldn't need to be concerned. Then our role is to talk to you about what has been said, and to explore with you what difficulties you might have and how we might be able to help you overcome them. Hopefully this helps you as a parent and helps your children as well.

Jake: This wasn't what happened to this friend of mine, no-one came to help her.

Worker: So the experience with your friend was that there was a lot of investigation and no help?

Jake: Yes, the child was taken away for a week, and brought back again, and then after about two months she didn't even hear or see anyone from child protection.

Worker: Sorry. I can't comment on what happened in that case because I don't know the family, I don't know the situation. All I can do is deal with you in this situation and tell you what my role is, and what we'll be doing with your family. And we prefer as much as possible to work together with families.

Jake: So can you help with things like babysitters and that sort of thing?

Worker: We can do a lot to help with getting referrals to services to get that sort of thing. There's a broad range of things that we can do. Part of it is ensuring the children's safety and part of it is to help you as a parent to look after your children.

Jake: Well, who's making this complaint?

Worker: I'm not allowed to tell you who has made the

complaint, that's protected information, but I can tell you what the information was that we were given in the report.

Jake: The neighbour next door. She would have done it. She doesn't like me.

Worker: I can't comment on who has or who hasn't made the complaint.

Jake: Well, she's mad, do you know that?

Worker: OK, you may feel that your neighbour did it. I can't say who has made the report, all I can say is what the concerns are, and then we can decide whether the concerns are real or not, and if there is some problem what we can do—how we can work together to resolve it.

Jake: How are you going to know if anything's happened? What's supposed to have happened anyway?

Worker: Well, the first thing we do is talk to you, we talk to your children, and we also would like to talk to some other professionals who might be involved or somebody else who might help us know what is happening with your children. Now we often talk with schools. They can tell us a lot about how things are with a family.

Jake: So you're going to be talking to the school about all this, are you?

Worker: If we can get your permission to talk to the school, that would be very helpful to us.

Jake: You won't talk to the school without my permission?

Worker: What we'll be doing first is asking for your permission to talk with the school. If it ever happens that a parent refuses permission to talk and we feel that we still need to, then I will tell you if we're going to do that.

Jake: So you can talk to the school anyway.

Worker: Not necessarily, it depends on the situation. Each situation is decided on its merits.

Jake: Can you tell me what the complaint is?

Worker: Yes, the concern is that you've been leaving your children, who I understand to be three and five, is that right? That you've been leaving them on their own at home for considerable periods of time—up to a couple of hours.

Jake: Well, that's not true.

Worker: So, does it ever happen? That they're left alone at home?

Jake: They are left at home for very short periods, when I need to do the shopping. I've got to feed them. I've had these children for the last two years, since the baby was still in nappies and their mother left two years ago. I've been doing all the work for them. I'm the one that's been changing the nappies, doing the shopping, doing the work.

Worker: And it's hard work.

Jake: Have you got children?

Worker: No, I haven't. I work with children and families a lot though and what I do know is that being a single parent, and looking after children on your own, is a very tough job. Being a parent is a tough job, but doing it on your own, when you haven't got backup, is even harder.

In this interview the worker is trying to help the client understand her welfare/investigatory role. By initially talking to the client about previous experiences, rather than launching into a description of her role, the worker is able to identify misapprehensions which the client might have about the role of the child protection worker and to deal with the client's fear that the children might be removed.

A second interview between a probation officer and an eighteen-year-old male client

In this case study the probation officer and client are exploring issues relating to appointments. The probation officer is trying to ensure that the probationer, Tom, understands what reporting as required means.

Probation officer (PO):   I would like to do a quick review of the probation order before we do anything else.

Tom: OK.

PO: Do you understand what is meant by being required to report to the probation officer as and when required?

Tom: Yes. It means I have to come here when you say so.

PO: That's right Tom. However, if you are unable to keep an appointment and you ring me up and give me an explanation then it might be OK to change the time of the appointment.

Tom: So if I want to go to the night football I could ring you?

PO: No. It would be most unusual for anyone to change an appointment because of a football match. You could ring and ask, however. That is the sort of thing that might be OK once you have established a regular pattern of reporting—perhaps after three or four months.

Tom: When can I miss appointments then?

PO: When it is something that might help you keep out of trouble or some sort of emergency—if you were asked to work overtime or if a family member was very ill. But you would still need to ring and let me know that you couldn't come.

Tom: What happens if I don't ring?

PO: You have been on probation before. What was your experience then?

Tom: The PO said I could not miss appointments but he did nothing about it when I did.

PO: Well I am different from that. If you miss an appointment without speaking to me first and you cannot provide a good explanation—for example, that you were sick and you have a doctor's certificate—then I give you a formal warning and that goes in the file. If you receive three formal warnings in the next six months, I have to refer to my senior probation officer who will make a decision whether to return the matter to court. Do you think you will have any problem keeping appointments?

Tom: I might, because I come here on a bus and sometimes the buses don't come.

PO: What could you do if that happened?

Tom: I guess I could ring you and make another time.

PO: That would be good. Could you bring in the bus timetable next time and I will try to schedule appointments so they fit in with the bus schedule?

Tom: OK.

PO: Are you likely to have any other problems keeping these appointments?

Tom: No. I don't think so.

This is a short excerpt and it seems mundane. To suggest that the worker is displaying role clarification skills in this interview might seem surprising. However, the research cited in this chapter and in Chapter 2 suggests that a willingness to explore these very practical issues with clients is related to positive outcomes. Probationers may develop misapprehensions about reporting requirements through previous experience, contact with other offenders or lack of information, and those misapprehensions can lead to failure to comply with the probation order. If the client understands what reporting as required means, and if he is given an opportunity to examine issues which might make it difficult for him to fulfil the requirements, he is likely to be in a better position to comply with the order and less likely to develop resentment which might arise from any misunderstanding.

The skill of role clarification for the most part is not complex. It is apparent, however, that when workers with involuntary clients devote time to it their clients do better.

SUMMARY

Direct practice with involuntary clients involves ongoing and frequent exploration with the client about the specific role of the worker and the part the client plays in the casework process. This chapter has highlighted a number of specific issues relating to role which should be addressed routinely in work with involuntary clients. These include: the dual (social control/welfare) role of the worker; what is negotiable and what is not negotiable and how the worker's authority might be used; the client's expectations of the worker; confidentiality and who has a right to information; the nature of the professional relationship and what this means in terms of how the worker and client interact; the role of the worker as case manager, case planner or problem solver/counsellor; the client's expectations of the casework process; the expectations the worker's employing organisation places on the worker and the client; and the theoretical approach the worker takes to the work.

Some of these issues are more relevant in some situations than others. It may not be appropriate, for example, to discuss all these issues in short-term contacts with involuntary clients. It does appear, however, that more effective workers devote time and energy to the clarification of role.

4 | Promoting pro-social outcomes

THE INTERVENTION MODEL presented in this book proposes that workers make use of the following skills in their work with involuntary clients: they work on ensuring that the client understands the role of the worker, particularly the dual social control (legalistic) and welfare role; they make use of the skills of pro-social modelling and reinforcement in order to encourage and promote client pro-social values and behaviours; they attempt to work with clients using a collaborative problem-solving approach which focuses on client definitions of problems and client goals; and they make use of relationship skills such as self-disclosure, empathy, optimism and humour. The model proposes that they use these skills in an explicit and open manner.

The pro-social approach (the use of pro-social modelling and reinforcement), like the other approaches described in this book, is based on the research about effective practice which shows it to be an effective method of working with involuntary clients (Andrews et al. 1979; Masters et al. 1987; Trotter 1996a). In fact in my study in corrections, it was clearly the most influential worker skill. Where workers made frequent use of the pro-social approach, their clients were imprisoned at about half the rate of clients of workers who made infrequent use of the approach, even after four years.

The approach is based on behaviourist theory. It is based on the belief that people are influenced by behaviour which is modelled by others and by positive and negative reinforcement of their own behaviour. A lot has been written, particularly in psychology, about behaviourist principles and their application to counselling situations.

Some basic behavioural principles include: behaviour is more likely to be maintained or developed if it is rewarded; the promise of a reward does not work as well as simply providing the actual reward following an occurrence of the particular behaviour; rewards are more effective if they are no greater than they need to be; rewards work best if they are perceived as fair in the circumstances; intrinsic rewards (those which exist in a client's natural environment) work best and foster continuation of the rewarded behaviour (Simons 1985); and variable rewards which provide reinforcement on an irregular basis are likely to be more effective than continuous or fixed ratio rewards (Hudson & McDonald 1986).

Whilst these principles are relevant to the pro-social approach, use of the approach does not require workers to have a detailed understanding of behaviourist theory. It simply involves a recognition that clients are likely to respond to modelling, rewards and punishments, and that workers should be aware of the nature of the models, rewards and punishments they offer.

The pro-social approach, as it was used in my study (Trotter 1996a) and the Andrews et al. (1979) study, asked workers to:

1. identify positive or pro-social comments or behaviours as they occurred in their interaction with clients;
2. reward those comments and behaviours wherever possible, most often by the use of praise;
3. present themselves as pro-social models; and
4. challenge anti-social or pro-criminal comments or behaviours.

The particular advantages and disadvantages of this approach are discussed later in this chapter. Outlined below is some more detail about the practical implementation of the approach using child protection work to illustrate it.

IDENTIFYING PRO-SOCIAL COMMENTS AND ACTIONS

During the course of interviews, workers should try to identify their client's pro-social comments and behaviours. This of course involves the worker thinking about the things that they would like their clients to be saying and doing.

In most cases what is a pro-social comment is fairly clear. Some examples include: comments by an abusive parent which recognise the harm that abuse of children can cause, or the harm that has been done by the specific behaviours of the parent; statements that recognise that children have feelings and developmental needs, for example, a comment by an abusive parent that her child was very upset after she was smacked; statements recognising the physical needs of children, for example, comments that babies' nappies should be changed regularly; statements recognising the role of the worker as one which has the interest of the child as a prime concern; comments which recognise that the client has a need for improved parenting skills; comments suggesting ways that parenting skills could be improved; or comments supporting a case plan developed in relation to the particular family. In some instances pro-social comments might also include interest in social activities or expressing interest in attending educational courses (e.g. for an isolated person).

Pro-social behaviours are along similar lines, for example: parents changing nappies regularly; using non-physical means to discipline children; undertaking a parenting skills course; arranging access with an estranged parent; talking to a child about feelings; showing interest in a child's schooling; attending an educational course; attending a case-planning meeting; or simply attending a meeting with the worker.

There are other instances when what is pro-social and what is not pro-social is more difficult to determine. Take, for example, a mother who has neglected her children and has now developed a relationship with a new boyfriend. She comments to the worker that her boyfriend is helping her to discipline her children and has smacked one of them. It may be a positive thing for the mother to have developed the relationship with the boyfriend and that the boyfriend is interested in the child. However, the worker may not wish to encourage the use of physical punishment, particularly by a new boyfriend.

Another example relates to a thirteen-year-old girl who has been admitted to care following numerous instances of running away from home. She approaches her worker saying that she wants to do something about birth control because she is worried that she could become pregnant. Again being concerned about not getting pregnant may be pro-social but having sexual relations at such a young age may not be.

Or again, a young offender comments to his worker that he is staying away from heroin but still uses marijuana for relaxation. Not using heroin may be pro-social but views might vary about the extent to which use of marijuana is pro-social.

Workers themselves hold a wide variety of views in relation

to various ethical issues. We have, no doubt, all worked or interacted with people with whom we strongly disagree on a range of moral and value-based issues. It could be that the use of the pro-social approach might lead to the imposition of particular values on clients by some workers. This issue is discussed later in the chapter. At this stage, however, I will look at the other steps in the pro-social approach.

PROVIDING REWARDS

The next step in the pro-social approach is to provide rewards or reinforcement for pro-social actions and comments. The most powerful reward or reinforcer available to the worker is praise. The pro-social approach involves the frequent use of praise for pro-social actions and comments. If, for example, a client attends a case-planning meeting, the social worker should make it clear that this is a good thing. Praise should be used liberally, but purposefully. It should be directed toward the pro-social comments and actions of the client. It should not simply be offered indiscriminately.

Attending for appointments, for example, is a pro-social action which should be rewarded. The idea would be to say to the client: 'It is good that you were able to get here on time today and that you have been able to get to our last couple of appointments; it is clear that you are taking the whole thing seriously', rather than simply saying: 'It is good to see you today.' The idea is to identify any pro-social acts or comments and praise them liberally, remembering, of course, that the praise is only likely to be effective if it appears to the client as genuine.

Again using the child protection example there are a number of rewards which might be used to encourage pro-social comments and actions. For example: visiting a client at home rather than the client visiting the office (or vice versa depending on the view of the client); referring the client to other resources; reducing the frequency of contact or in some instances spending more time with clients; visiting at times the client chooses; organising financial assistance; or organising practical assistance for a client, such as home maintenance, furniture or transport.

A good illustration of the way in which rewards can be used to reinforce behaviour relates to the place in which an interview is held. In deciding to conduct an interview in McDonald's, for example, rather than in the worker's office the worker is providing a reward to the client (particularly if the client also gets a free lunch). If the client is left to think that this is simply routine then an opportunity is lost. Rather, using the pro-social approach, the worker would make it clear that the interview is being conducted away from the office because the client prefers this. The worker would point out that she is happy to put herself out in this way because the client has kept appointments regularly, has followed up a referral to a parenting group and is openly discussing problems with the worker. The client in this instance gets a sense that doing the things that the worker wants will help to get what she (the client) wants.

Taking the converse situation of a client who is not reporting regularly and is being generally uncooperative—if the worker in this instance decides to see the client in McDonald's in the hope that the client will be more cooperative, and this is in some way communicated to the client, then the client can get a sense that her uncooperative behaviour has led to a reward. The uncooperative behaviour is reinforced and is more likely to continue.

A qualitative study undertaken in corrections found that workers often inadvertently reinforced the very things they were trying to prevent (Burns 1994). For example, one worker made the following comment: 'We are getting nowhere with these interviews and I think we should see each other less often in the future.' This comment represents a clear reward for uncooperative (not pro-social) behaviour.

It is sometimes argued in seminars I have conducted that these things are rights rather than rewards and should not be dispensed as rewards. However, in reality workers make discretionary decisions about these issues on a day-to-day basis. If clients feel that the worker is just as likely to reward them if they make anti-social or pro-criminal comments then their anti-social behaviour is more likely to continue. On the other hand, if it is clear to the client that positive behaviours and attitudes can lead to the things they want, then they are more likely to make use of them.

The role of the worker is to ensure that the reward system works in this way. In many cases it is simply a matter of the worker being explicit about the reasons for a particular action being taken. If the frequency of contact is reduced, for example, then it is generally because of progress of some sort on the part of the client. It is simply a matter of making this explicit.

Another method by which clients can be rewarded is through

the use of file notes or letters. Workers might make notes about the positive things that clients have done and share these with the client. It might be highlighted in file notes, for example, that the client has kept appointments regularly, attended for case-planning meetings, followed up referrals for drug rehabilitation, and consequently the frequency of contact with the worker is to be reduced. Letters might also be written to clients between sessions, a strategy recommended in narrative therapy (White & Epston 1989), in order to reinforce the positive steps which clients have made. Similarly, final reports or final letters to clients can be used to highlight the pro-social actions of clients.

Through the reinforcement process it appears that clients learn the behaviours and attitudes which the worker is trying to promote. It is apparent from research with offenders that the learned behaviours are learned quickly (within a few months), and sustained over the long term. As mentioned earlier, reduced reoffending rates, following the use of this approach in probation supervision, continued to be seen in my study even after four years despite the fact that supervision for the most part ceased within one year (Trotter 1996a).

MODELLING PRO-SOCIAL BEHAVIOURS

The third aspect of the pro-social approach relates to modelling pro-social behaviours. Modelling pro-social behaviours involves the worker modelling the behaviour that she wishes to foster in the client. Again using child protection to illustrate the principle, the worker should be available when she is supposed to be, or ring to change appointments; she should treat the family with the same respect with which she hopes the family members will treat their children; she should speak positively about her own children; she should express views about the importance of children receiving good care; show empathy for the children's situation and similarly show empathy for the parents' situation (without condoning antisocial behaviours in any way).

Some degree of self-disclosure may be appropriate in presenting as a pro-social model. For example, a worker might comment on how difficult she found it when her children were young although she always managed to avoid using physical punishment. In this type of modelling it is important not to appear to be smug or have all the answers. In fact a useful distinction is sometimes made between 'coping' modelling as opposed to modelling which suggests that the worker has all the answers (Masters et al. 1987). Coping modelling, which reveals the worker's vulnerability and which acknowledges the difficulty which the worker has experienced, seems to work better.

The appropriateness of self-disclosure is discussed in Chapters 2 and 6. It is very difficult to be prescriptive about it, nonetheless, it does appear that self-disclosure is one method of modelling and encouraging particular behaviours. Masters et al. (1987), for example, refer to studies suggesting that worker self-disclosure leads to client self-disclosure. Similarly, as discussed in Chapters 2 and 6, it is important to model an optimistic approach to the work, a belief in your capacity to help and in the client's capacity to change.

CHALLENGING UNDESIRABLE BEHAVIOURS

The fourth aspect of this model relates to the challenging of anti-social or undesirable behaviours or comments. Anti-social comments include attempts by the client to rationalise their anti-social behaviour. Examples from child protection include: 'I was only disciplining her'; 'I only hit him because he kept crying'; 'A good whack did not do me any harm when I was a child and shouldn't harm anyone today'; or 'I would change the nappies more often if I had a washing machine that worked'.

The child protection worker should identify comments such as these as rationalisations for behaviours which have led the person to become a client of protective services, and then provide some level of negative reinforcement for them. This might include ignoring the behaviour, pointing out that the worker does not agree with the comments or simply expressing the view that they are, in fact, rationalisations for unacceptable behaviour.

Care should be taken not to positively reinforce anti-social comments through the inadvertent use of body language, as occurred in many cases in a study of the use of pro-social approaches in probation by Patrick Burns (1994). Burns found that probation officers often inadvertently reinforced anti-social and pro-criminal comments through the use of body language (e.g. smiling).

Workers should be careful not to respond to rationalisations or anti-social comments with exclusively empathic comments. Whilst rationalisations will inevitably contain some truth (coping with dirty nappies without a washing machine is very difficult, as is coping with crying babies in general), it is important that they are not accepted by the worker as excuses for the behaviour. It must be clear to the client that whilst the worker might understand, the worker does not approve of the excuses for anti-social behaviour.

Whilst it is important that the client understands that the worker does not approve of rationalisations or anti-social comments or actions, it is also important that disapproval and confrontation does not overwhelm the direct practice intervention. This aspect of the pro-social approach needs to be used with some caution. It has been suggested in the corrections area, albeit rather arbitrarily, that workers should try to provide at least four positive comments for every negative one (Keissling 1982). The model as it was implemented in my research (Trotter 1993, 1996a) focused strongly on positives rather than negatives. The Australian qualitative study by Burns referred to above also found that more successful probation officers focused almost exclusively on positives in contrast with less successful officers who were more inclined to focus on negatives.

The need for caution in relation to use of negative reinforcement and confrontation is supported by Shulman, who states in relation to confrontation that:

> . . . analysis of the data on the skills of confrontation thought to be crucial to effective social work practice did not yield the expected supporting results. When it occurs seems to be important. Confrontation which comes too early in the relationship or which is not balanced by a large amount of positive comment may well have a negative impact. (Shulman 1991:11)

To sum up, it is important in work with involuntary clients that pro-social comments and behaviour are rewarded. It is also important that clients understand that the worker does not approve of anti-social behaviour or rationalisations for it. However, it should also be remembered that people are more likely to learn from positive reinforcement and workers should focus on the positives.

Case example

It is interesting to consider the example which was raised in the introduction about clients who come to the office at a time different from their scheduled appointment. On the one hand, workers can argue that they should be sent away because the client should learn responsibility. On the other hand, other workers can argue that the client should be seen because it is respectful. What approach should someone take who was using the principles of pro-social modelling and reinforcement?

Let's assume that you as the worker wish to encourage the client for coming to see you. However, you do not wish to encourage turning up at unexpected times because it is inconvenient for you. You wish of course to model behaviour which is consistent with the behaviour you are seeking from your client. Therefore you talk to the client as promptly as possible. You explain to the client that you are pleased to see him and that you appreciate the fact that he has made the effort to come and see you. You attempt to reward his pro-social action in coming to the office and you model respectful behaviour in talking to the client as soon as possible. You then explain to the client that this is an inconvenient time and you make another appointment. It is likely that the client will remember the correct appointment next time.

If, on the other hand, you interview the client at the unscheduled time this will reward his behaviour in turning up unexpectedly and the behaviour is likely to occur again.

In other situations it might be appropriate to focus on the client's pro-social behaviour in coming to see the worker. Some intellectually disabled, psychiatrically ill or drug-using clients might have difficulty with appointment times. The visit might represent a breakthrough in work with a resistant client. In such an instance it may be appropriate to see the client and praise the client for attending. This is likely to encourage the client to attend again, although not at the scheduled time.

The worker must think through this issue and decide what behaviour she wishes to encourage. In the first example the worker defines the pro-social behaviour as attending at the scheduled time. In the second example it is defined as simply attending.

ADVANTAGES OF THE PRO-SOCIAL APPROACH

The greatest strength of the pro-social approach is that the research evidence suggests that it works. It seems to be related to client outcomes with a range of involuntary clients. The evidence from my study in corrections (Trotter 1993) found also that the use of the approach significantly correlated with a number of client satisfaction measures. The success of this approach can also be explained theoretically by reference to behaviour theory.

The pro-social approach seems to work because it provides a method for discouraging and challenging anti-social comments and behaviours within a positive framework. It puts into practice the idea that people learn best by encouragement rather than discouragement.

The approach also helps workers to take control of a reinforcement process which occurs anyway. Whether they are aware of it or not workers with involuntary clients do make judgements about the things they wish to encourage in their clients, and they do in turn influence their clients' behaviour (Andrews et al. 1979; Burns 1994; Trotter 1990, 1996a). By understanding the process and using this approach workers are able to take more control over the nature of this influence.

CRITICISMS OF THE PRO-SOCIAL APPROACH

Behaviourist approaches have not generally been popular in welfare circles. Two of the few recent publications to refer to it are *Behavioural Social Work* by B.L. Hudson and G.M. McDonald, published in 1986, and Ronald Rooney's 1992 book on involuntary clients, which devotes a chapter to influencing behaviours and attitudes. On the whole, however, few social work or welfare texts discuss how workers influence client behaviours through the reinforcement and modelling process. In fact, there continues to be criticism of behaviourist approaches in some welfare circles (e.g. Ife 1997). Outlined below are responses to some of the questions and criticisms which are sometimes raised in relation to the pro-social approach.

What if clients make pro-social comments but their behaviour is inconsistent with their comments?

The aim of the pro-social approach is to reward pro-social behaviour and comments, that is, comments and behaviour which are honest and genuine. A dishonest or frivolous array of comments by an involuntary client about how he has changed should not be defined as pro-social and should not be rewarded, particularly if those comments are not consistent with the client's behaviour.

That said, it can be difficult to determine whether someone is genuine or not. The worker clearly needs to avoid being 'conned' and should avoid reinforcing behaviour which attempts to do this. Nonetheless, if in doubt, it seems that the most appropriate approach is to accept the client's word—at least until the worker has firm information that what the client is saying is incorrect.

Don't workers do this anyway?

One of the most frequent comments made in my workshops when this material is presented is 'I do it anyway'. Some workers feel that the pro-social approach merely describes a process which they use unconsciously. However, there is evidence that those who work with involuntary clients do not routinely use these skills. The Canadian corrections study (Andrews et al. 1979) and the Australian studies (Burns 1994; Trotter 1990, 1993, 1996a) found that probation officers, many of whom were trained in social work and welfare, used the pro-social approach very erratically. Some probation officers used it and some did not. There was also a clear change in the behaviour of probation officers after they completed training in the use of the approach. As mentioned earlier, Burns' qualitative study undertaken in corrections in Victoria, Australia, found that many probation officers inadvertently reinforced the very behaviour they were hoping to change, often through the use of smiling and body language as much as direct comment or actions (Burns 1994).

There seems little doubt that whilst pro-social skills might come naturally to some workers they do not come naturally to everyone and they can be increased with training and by an awareness of them.

One of the strongest arguments in favour of the pro-social approach relates to this notion that it occurs anyway. It seems that whether they are conscious of it or not, to one degree or another, workers reinforce different behaviours in their clients. It is preferable that they are explicit about this process both with themselves and their clients and that they take some control over it.

Is this approach superficial?

It might also be argued that the approach is superficial and symptom-focused, and it is therefore unlikely to address the complex long-term problems of involuntary clients. How could such an approach address issues relating to poverty, unemployment, drug use, depression, and so on? It is certainly true that the pro-social approach will not address all the problems of involuntary clients. It is, however, one skill which relates to client outcomes and which can be used along with a range of other skills that might address underlying problems.

Clients can be influenced by the positive and negative reactions of workers, and an understanding of the process, and constructive use of the skills involved can facilitate movement toward both worker goals and client goals. This process might be superficial but the evidence suggests it is influential.

Is this approach manipulative?

The pro-social approach could be viewed as manipulative inasmuch as it attempts to change the behaviour of clients in directions set by the worker rather than the client. On the other hand, workers inevitably manipulate clients by encouraging and discouraging certain behaviours. It is far better that this manipulation be explicit than implicit, and that the client and the social worker understand the process.

To ensure that the process is fair it is particularly important that the worker is open about it. The worker should explain to the client what it involves. The worker should be clear about the goals she is pursuing and how these might differ from the client's goals. The worker should explain how the reinforcement process will be used to facilitate the achievement of both worker and client goals. As pointed out earlier, effective work with involuntary clients involves an honest and open approach from the worker in relation to issues of authority and role. Where this is present the pro-social approach is, I believe, less manipulative than traditional approaches with involuntary clients where manipulation may be hidden.

Doesn't effective practice involve a focus on client goals?

Chapter 2 pointed to a number of research studies which suggested that agreement on goals between client and worker is important to effective practice with both voluntary and involuntary clients. Yet the pro-social approach suggests that change can be achieved when workers and clients have different goals.

Wherever possible, workers should work with client goals. In fact, the overriding aim of direct practice, whether or not a pro-social approach is being used, whether clients are involuntary or not, is to reach agreement on goals and if possible work with client goals. In many instances in work with involuntary clients agreement can be reached about goals. However, workers are often confronted with a situation where the client has been referred for behaviours or problems which are either denied or minimised. In fact, in my experience many workers would say this situation is all too common.

In these instances the worker has certain options: one is to work with the client on goals which the client chooses; another is to be up front about the goals of the worker and the organisation, and to make it explicit that any progress toward these goals will be rewarded and reinforced; another is a combination of the two. This third option is consistent with the practice model presented in this book.

In this case the worker might work with the goals as defined by the client, where these goals are not in conflict with worker goals. At the same time the worker would simultaneously reinforce progress toward worker and agency goals, such as stopping child abuse, or offending, or domestic violence. The pro-social approach may be used in this way simultaneously with the problem-solving process (see Chapter 5).

In one way or another in work with involuntary clients workers have to deal with the issue of the different goals held by many of their clients and themselves. The pro-social approach provides a method of doing this.

Is this approach judgemental?

Much of the direct practice literature suggests that caseworkers should be non-judgemental (e.g. Heffernan et al. 1997). Yet the pro-social approach is based on value judgements. The term 'pro-social' has connotations of social control, of there being a right way of doing things, or that what is socially acceptable is best.

Workers with involuntary clients are employed by the state to work with people who have been judged to have transgressed social mores. On a day-to-day basis they make judgements about what are unacceptable standards of parenting or what are acceptable levels of drug use or violence. Direct practice workers make these judgements, they communicate them to clients and they in turn influence clients' behaviours. It should be noted that the corrections studies referred to earlier (Andrews et al. 1979; Trotter 1990, 1993) suggest that workers reinforce different expressions and behaviours regardless of whether they have any awareness of doing so.

Nonetheless it is important that pro-social behaviour be defined in explicit and limited terms. It should not be interpreted as meaning having values consistent with the worker. In child protection, for example, it should be defined specifically in terms of behaviours and expressions or attitudes which are consistent with the aim of providing a safe environment for children. As discussed earlier, the Canadian study in corrections (Andrews et al. 1979) unlike the Australian studies (Trotter 1990, 1993) found that supervisors who practised the pro-social approach were only effective if they also practised reflective listening and had high levels of empathy.

It does seem that if the pro-social approach is in any way used as an excuse for moralising on the part of the worker it is not going to work. Perhaps one of the strongest arguments for focusing on positives is that it is likely to avoid the possibility that the pro-social approach will come across as moralistic and disapproving.

Working with involuntary clients involves working in a value-laden environment. What is needed is a recognition that this is so and debate about how the ethical and value-based issues should be dealt with. One of the aims of the pro-social approach is to provide a framework within which these value-based issues can be addressed.

Is the pro-social approach consistent with feminist casework?

Direct practice with involuntary clients is sometimes criticised because it is seen as supporting the status quo. Many books and articles have been written favouring an approach to casework which seeks to change social stereotypes and disadvantage in addition to helping individuals deal with problems (e.g. Fook 1993).

It is argued in Chapter 5 that some of these issues can be addressed through the problem-solving process. It was also argued in Chapter 2 that the practice model presented in this book can facilitate a feminist approach to casework. The pro-social approach, in particular, provides a framework within which feminist or radical casework principles can be made explicit and promoted. For example, a probation officer might be working with an offender who is on probation for a domestic violence offence and who has a negative attitude toward women. The probation officer, consistent with the pro-social approach, would express a goal of changing the client's sexist attitudes. This would be seen as consistent with the overall goal of reduced offending. The probation officer would challenge any sexist comments or rationalisations for sexist behaviour, model non-sexist behaviour and reinforce and reward non-sexist comments made by the client. Similarly, using a pro-social approach a feminist worker working with a female client who lives within a patriarchal family setting would reinforce any comments that the client made which reflected an awareness of her disadvantage as a woman and challenge comments which reflected an acceptance of patriarchal values. The worker would encourage and reward the identification of goals which helped the client to develop independence.

Is the pro-social approach appropriate across cultures?

Definitions of what is and what is not pro-social are inevitably entrenched in social and cultural mores. For example, female circumcision may be legal and acceptable in one culture yet illegal and immoral in another. In one country it might be common practice to inflict severe physical punishments on criminal offenders whereas in another country such practices would be illegal. A family might have a cultural tradition which does not allow young women to go out in the evenings unchaperoned, but the young female client of that family might feel strongly that this is inappropriate. Whilst a worker might define these restrictions on the young person as not pro-social, the parents might argue that the restrictions are pro-social within their culture.

Workers and clients are influenced by their racial, social, religious and economic milieux. Both workers and clients often have strong beliefs about which behaviours might be viewed as pro-social. Who is to decide in these instances what is pro-social and what isn't?

In using the pro-social approach certain principles should apply to guard against this approach becoming a disguise for workers to be moralising and self-righteous. The approach should not provide a method of imposing workers' values on clients.

First, workers should focus on positives. This has been emphasised several times and is vital to the effective use of this approach.

Second, confrontation and challenging client behaviour and comments should be limited to factors which relate to the presenting problem (or the mandate for the worker's involvement with the client). For the most part, in the involuntary context, this relates to illegal behaviour, for example, offending, domestic violence, truancy or child abuse.

Other 'desirable' behaviours which the worker may wish to encourage, such as seeking employment, developing a relationship, returning to study, developing a more equitable interaction with a partner or visiting estranged children should be encouraged if the worker believes they are pro-social. The client's failure to do these things should not, however, result in confrontation by the worker.

Third, the direct practice worker should attempt to understand the views and actions of clients in terms of their cultural context. In forming views about what is pro-social in any given situation the worker should take the client's cultural background into account. This involves talking to the client about cultural differences.

Fourth, workers should examine their own beliefs regarding what is pro-social and what is not, and be explicit about these views with themselves and their clients.

Clients should have the option to choose another worker when there are differences in values which make working together too difficult.

CASE EXAMPLE—A PERPETRATOR OF DOMESTIC VIOLENCE WHO HAS BEEN PLACED ON PROBATION

Con was placed on probation following an assault on his wife which resulted in her hospitalisation and their subsequent separation. This is the third interview between the probation officer and Con, who has now returned to live with his wife.

> *PO:* It is good to see you. I appreciate your coming on time. It does make things easier for me. Did you come on public transport?
> *Con:* Yes. I lost my licence a few months ago.
> *PO:* Well, I am pleased to hear that you are not driving. Did you come by train?
> *Con:* Train and bus.
> *PO:* How long did that take?
> *Con:* More than an hour. The bus was late.
> *PO:* As I said, I appreciate you making it on time. It has obviously taken some effort. You were saying in the last interview you were thinking of going back home?

Con: I am back home now.

PO: When did you go home?

Con: Last week.

PO: How does your wife feel about it?

Con: She asked me to come back. She seems all right as long as I keep attending the [domestic violence] groups.

PO: I have spoken to the group convener. He said you have been attending but you did miss the first meeting. You have been to two out of three. You seem to be taking this whole thing seriously—attending the groups and coming to these appointments. It is a pity you missed the first one. You must attend eight of the ten sessions or you will have to do the program again.

Con: I did not know that.

PO: I mentioned it last week. Is it a problem?

Con: No. I have to go because of her anyway.

PO: So you are motivated to attend the groups because of your wife's feelings about it?

Con: She'll probably ring the cops again if I don't go.

PO: The main thing is that you are planning to continue to attend the groups. That is good. Can we talk a bit about the groups? How are you finding them?

Con: They are OK. We mostly seem to talk about our feelings or have little lectures about violence.

PO: So are you finding them useful?

Con: They are OK. Anyway I know what will happen if I hit her again. Not that I ever did anything more than give her a bit of a slap. But she says if I ever hit her again that will be the end.

PO: I understand from reading the police report that you injured your wife quite badly. It certainly was not a bit of a slap. However, I am pleased to hear you say that you will not hit you wife again. Does she mean a lot to you?

Con: She does and I did not want to hit her but she makes me so angry. She says things just to make me mad.

PO: You know and I know that that is no excuse for hitting her. Are you saying that you have decided to change your behaviour toward your wife?

Con: Well, I know now that I just cannot do it again.

PO: I am pleased to hear you say that. I think you are doing pretty well on probation. You have kept most of the appointments and you seem to be determined not to repeat this offence. Seeing you have been doing well I would be quite happy to come to your house for the next appointment. This will give me a chance to talk to your wife again. In the meantime I will ring her about how things are going and about the assistance she is receiving. Now, let's talk more about the situation at home.

In this interview the worker is trying to praise each pro-social comment or action by Con. She praises his punctual attendance, his not driving whilst his licence is suspended, the effort he has taken to get to the interview, the attendance at two of the domestic violence groups and his motivation to continue attending because of his wife's wishes, his apparent changed behaviour with his wife, and his assertion that he will not hit her again. The probation officer offers to visit the client at home for the next visit which will save the client a lot of time and effort. She links this to his good response to probation.

She also makes it clear that she does not approve of a number of Con's comments and actions. These include the missed domestic violence group and the minimisation of the violence toward his wife. The worker also makes it clear that she plans to talk to Con's wife about her current situation.

In this example it is likely that the worker strongly disapproves of the offence which the client has committed and of the client's rationalisations for his behaviour. Nonetheless, consistent with the pro-social approach, the worker focuses on positives whilst at the same time making it clear that she does not approve of the offence and does not accept the rationalisations. She focuses on positives on the understanding that this is more likely to lead to changes in the client's behaviour than an approach which focuses on what the client has done wrong.

SUMMARY

The pro-social approach is one of four key skills which comprise the empirical intervention model presented in this book—the others being role clarification, problem solving and relationship skills. The pro-social approach involves four steps: identifying client pro-social comments and actions; rewarding those comments and actions; presenting oneself as a pro-social model; and challenging anti-social or pro-criminal comments and actions.

The pro-social approach has a number of advantages as an intervention method. Its greatest advantage is that a number of research studies have pointed to its effectiveness in improving client outcomes. A number of criticisms are sometimes made of the pro-social approach. These include that clients may say pro-social things but not do them, workers use this approach anyway, the approach is superficial, manipulative, judgemental and does not focus on client goals. Each of these criticisms has been addressed in this chapter. How the approach fits with some different perspectives from feminist casework to casework across cultures was also discussed.

5 | Problem solving

PROBLEM-SOLVING APPROACHES have been popular in welfare and helping situations for many years. Helen Harris Perlman (1957) developed a problem-solving model for work in welfare settings more than 40 years ago. William Reid and Laura Epstein published *Task-centred Casework* in 1972, which also outlined a problem-solving model for casework practice. These models have since been further refined (e.g. Reid & Epstein 1977; Doel & Marsh 1992; Reid 1992). Problem solving has been adapted for use in probation by Jerry Keissling (1982), and for use with other involuntary clients by Ronald Rooney (1992). Variations on the problem-solving model have also been developed in psychological rather than welfare settings (e.g. Carkhuff 1969). Most current social work and welfare texts continue to include material on problem-solving approaches (e.g. Compton & Galaway 1994; Hepworth et al. 1997).

The problem-solving model presented in this chapter makes use of much of the material presented in these publications. However, it relates this material specifically to work with involuntary clients. It also attempts to integrate principles of assessment, case planning and case management into the problem-solving framework. The model incorporates the principles related to effective outcomes in work with involuntary clients referred to in Chapter 2. The model has been tested and further developed in my research in probation and child protection (Trotter 1996a, 1997c).

STEPS IN THE PROBLEM-SOLVING PROCESS

The model includes seven steps: (1) problem survey; (2) problem ranking; (3) problem exploration; (4) setting goals; (5) developing a contract; (6) developing strategies and tasks; and (7) ongoing review and monitoring.

It should be stated at the outset that whilst workers are encouraged to work through the steps of the model as systematically as possible, in many instances this is not possible. In work with many involuntary clients, particularly those with drug-abuse problems, psychiatric illness or intellectual disability, working sequentially may be difficult. People's problems or their perceptions of them may change from one week to the next or in some instances from one minute to the next. So in practice workers might find they move back and forth in relation to the various stages of the model. It is important, nonetheless, that the model is used to provide a clear structure for the interaction between the worker and client, and that the worker tries to work through the model sequentially, as far as possible.

The client should be given information about the nature of the problem-solving process. As mentioned earlier some of the workers in child protection and probation I have worked with have the steps of the problem-solving process in large print on a poster on their office wall. They are then able to show this to their clients, explain it to them, and regularly identify the stage they are at in relation to the process. This is certainly an approach I favour because it facilitates an open partnership approach. An example of the charts which workers have used is included in the Appendix.

Problem survey

The problem survey, the first step in the problem-solving process, begins after the initial role clarification. Its purpose is to gain a picture of the clients' perception of the situation and the issues of concern to them. It sets the stage for further ongoing work with clients in relation to their problems.

What is involved in the problem survey?
What is involved at this stage is straightforward. Clients are simply asked to list or identify any problems they may have. The worker might ask the client to identify anything in her life which she would like to change. The use of questions similar to those used

in solution-focused counselling (e.g. Berg & DeJong 1996) may help to identify problems. For example, 'What would be different if everything was the way you wanted it to be?'

The aim is to get a written list of things the client is unhappy about or would like to change. In developing this list the worker might work through an assessment framework which might be in use in the particular organisation. If no such framework is available, the worker might simply work through areas such as employment, housing, family situation, drug use, recreation and finances.

The list should be written down, on a white board or on a piece of paper and be viewed as the client's list of issues. The client is the final arbiter of what is included on the list and what is not included. The worker should, however, encourage the client to identify problems which the worker feels are related to the behaviour which has led the client to become a client.

As the client identifies different problems, the worker should ask the client to talk about each problem. Why is it a problem? How severe is the problem? How long has it been going on? For example, in relation to a problem of unemployment, the worker might seek to clarify with the client how long she has been unemployed; how she feels about this; whether she has worked previously; how she fills in her days.

It may be appropriate to break a problem down, or partialise the problem, at this stage. For example, a client may say she is depressed and the worker may seek to partialise different aspects of this problem: Is the depression related to specifics like accommodation or lack of relationships? Does it involve an inability to get out of bed in the mornings? Is the client suicidal?

It is important that the problems are listed in the client's terms and in the client's language. This is the client's list. If the client has a problem with 'no work' or a 'very small house', the problem should be written down in these terms rather than as 'unemployment' and 'inadequate accommodation'. The worker may rephrase problem definitions in order to be clear about what is being said. For example, the worker might say, 'You mean this house is not big enough for you and two children'. However, the problem list should as far as possible be the client's expression of the problem in the client's words.

As discussed later in this chapter, problem-solving approaches are sometimes criticised because of the focus on problems rather than strengths. Steve DeShazer (1988), in his work on solution-focused approaches, refers to complaints rather than problems.

Dorothy Scott and Di O'Neill (1996), in their work on solution-focused approaches in child protection, refer to 'issues which currently concern the family'. I argue later that problem solving is not a negative experience for clients, nonetheless referring to problems as issues or things the client would like to change may help to make the problem survey less negative and less overwhelming for the client.

Problem ranking

Once the problem survey has been completed, in other words, once the worker and the client have developed a list of problems or issues from the client's perspective, then a decision should be made about which problems to work on. Generally it is appropriate to start with one or perhaps two manageable issues.

In work with involuntary clients there are a number of guidelines for deciding with the client which issues to work on. To begin with, there will sometimes be crisis situations which need immediate action, often before the worker has had time to work through the problem-survey or problem-ranking process. For example, there could be a crisis which requires the immediate placement of children, or immediate hospitalisation of a drug user or a mentally ill client. Obviously these situations will take priority.

Next, the problem to work on must be one which the client agrees is a problem. The worker may suggest that a particular problem is a good one to start with and give the client reasons for this. However, it is vital that the client views the problem as a problem.

It is also best to start with problems which have a good chance of being resolved. Some immediate success at the beginning of the problem-solving process provides an incentive to both worker and client. For example, it may not be appropriate to start with a housing problem if the worker is aware of a severe housing shortage in the area. There may be more chance of success if the worker and the client decide to work on a problem relating to a client being housebound with her young children. It may be that the worker is familiar with good daycare for children or it may be that the client has relatives who could assist.

If resources are available to help solve the problem there is more chance of achieving short-term success. It is of course very helpful at this stage if the worker has a good working knowledge of relevant resources.

Whilst it is vital that the problem to be worked on is a real problem from the client's perspective, the worker should encourage the client to work on problems which are related to the reason the client is a client. For example, an offender may wish to work on a problem relating to her relationship with a drug-using partner. The worker, however, might feel that the partner has a negative influence on the client and leads her to greater use of drugs. The worker might therefore encourage the client to work on a problem relating to her drug use rather than the problem with her relationship.

If the worker feels strongly that the problem the client has chosen is not the most appropriate one to work on then it may be appropriate to suggest to the client that two problems be worked on simultaneously. The client and worker might agree, for example, to address both the drug problem and the relationship problem. Nonetheless, it remains vital that the client does view both problems as real problems.

The worker may also encourage the client to work on problems and goals in a manner which is consistent with pro-social values. For example, a male client who has been a perpetrator of domestic violence may have a problem with what he perceives as his partner's lack of support. He may want his partner to carry out more tasks around the home and generally be more supportive of him. The worker may feel that working on such a problem would be supporting a patriarchal view on the client's part. In this instance the worker would discourage the client from working on this problem.

Finally, the focus of this problem-solving model should be on practical rather than intra-psychic issues. The research in relation to psychoanalytic approaches in work with involuntary clients is not positive (Alexander & Parsons 1973; Fischer 1973; Wood 1978; Rubin 1985; Videka Sherman 1988; Gough 1993; Andrews & Bonta 1994). When clients raise non-specific problems such as depression, low self-esteem, anxiety or guilt, for example, they should be broken down into more tangible concerns. A client who expresses concern about feeling bad about herself and having low self-esteem might be asked to talk about why she has low self-esteem. It might be possible to relate this to not having friends, not having work, feeling stigmatised by being on a court order, and feeling inadequate because she has no money. Rather than dealing with the non-specific issue of low self-esteem, the worker and the client might choose to work on one of these more specific problems.

FROM MY OWN direct practice work and from workshops I have conducted with practising professionals, it is apparent that the time it takes to work through the problem survey and problem-ranking stages of the problem-solving process is unpredictable. In some instances it is possible to work through these steps in one or two interviews. In other cases it may take longer. It is not uncommon to work through the problem survey over as many as five or six interviews, move on to the next stage of the process and still have to return to the problem survey stage weeks later.

For example, in one instance I worked through the various stages of the problem-solving process with a young probationer whom I believed was alcoholic. Despite my attempts to raise the issue he consistently refused to identify his drinking as a problem for him. We worked on a number of other issues including his family relationships. On one occasion after some months as he was about to leave the office he commented that he was worried because he had been drinking too much and this was what got him into trouble last time. We were then able to resume the interview and go back to the problem survey stage of the problem-solving process. The client then began to explore this issue and to develop some strategies to address his fears that he might repeat his offence.

Problem exploration

Some problem exploration will have already occurred during the problem survey stage. Nonetheless once the worker has decided which problem to work on it can be helpful to do some more exploration of the problem and factors which might impact on it. In some cases this problem exploration might lead to a different definition of the problem.

The client should be asked to talk about how the problem began, when it began, what factors are preventing its solution, whether attempts have been made to solve the problem, and how successful they have been.

For example, a probation officer might be working with a young probationer and between them they have agreed to work on the problem of the probationer's lack of employment. The probation officer then begins to explore this issue. He would want to know about how long the young person had been unemployed; if she had ever worked; if so in what type of work; how long she remained in the job; whether she left the job voluntarily or was asked to leave; what the specific circumstances of her leaving were; whether she is seeking other work; if so, what type; whether she has been for interviews; whether she uses newspapers or word of mouth to find out about positions; what education or skills she has; how she presents for interviews; and so on.

Some of this material will have been covered in the problem survey stage, however the aim at this stage of the process is to learn as much as possible about the problem and the surrounding issues. It could become evident as the problem is explored that before it can be resolved other issues need to be addressed. For example, a young person might be seeking work which requires some skill or training they don't have. The problem might need to be redefined as inadequate skills to find the type of work which she wants. This might lead to an exploration of her skills and possible training opportunities.

Jerry Keissling (1982), in his work in probation, suggests that probation officers should spend as long as they feel they need in the problem exploration stage and then spend some more time. In other words, it is very important to gain an understanding of the problem and its context at this stage. For example, there may be little point working on a plan for seeking employment if the client lives in an isolated area with no access to transport. This means that in the midst of the problem exploration it might be necessary to return to the problem survey and problem-ranking stages of the process. The worker and the client might agree to work initially on the problem of geographical isolation rather than immediately addressing the problem of employment. The problem exploration stage would then begin for the second time.

When the worker is satisfied that he has a clear picture of the problem in its broad context then the worker and the client should attempt to define what exactly the client wants to happen. In other words, what are the client's goals?

Setting goals

It was pointed out in Chapter 2 that agreement on goals between worker and client consistently emerges in the research as being related to positive outcomes with both voluntary and involuntary clients (Rubin 1985; Sheldon 1987; Videka Sherman 1988). The development of goals is about the worker and the client reaching agreement on what they are trying to achieve together.

The worker and client may well have different interpretations of the goals. These different interpretations can sometimes be subtle. It is important therefore that goals are defined in specific terms and as far as possible leave little scope for different interpretations. Thus it is important that the specific goals are written down and a copy is available to both the worker and the client.

Examples of goals include:

- for Melinda to find part-time employment in a sales position within six weeks;
- for Melinda to obtain new accommodation with at least two bedrooms which is within walking distance of the city centre, or which is less than ten minutes' walk from a train or bus which goes at least every 30 minutes to the city centre;
- for Melinda to have regular contact (at least once a week for 30 minutes) with another woman who lives in her area;
- for Ben (aged seven) to stop hitting his sister (aged five) within one week.

Some examples of goals which are not sufficiently specific and which might lead to uncertainty include:

- for Melinda to get a job;
- for Melinda to find new accommodation;
- for Melinda to make friends;
- for Ben to treat his sister better.

Developing a contract

At this stage, after the problems have been identified through the problem survey, ranked, further explored and goals set, a written contract is developed with the purpose of summarising these steps for the benefit of the worker and the client. Ideally the contract, as a summary of client problems and goals, should be written by the client. In practice, however, contracts are most often written by the worker in collaboration with the client. An example of a contract is outlined on page 93.

Developing strategies and tasks

The next step in the problem-solving process is the development of tasks or strategies to achieve the goals. This is sometimes referred to as 'developing solutions'.

Problem-solving contract

Problems

1. Melinda has no work.
2. Melinda's house is too small for her and two children.
3. Melinda has no friends.
4. Melinda is worried about the violent behaviour of Ben (seven years) towards his sister Maeve (five years).

Initially it is agreed to work on the third and fourth problems.

Goals

1. For Melinda to have regular contact (at least once a week for 30 minutes) with another woman who lives in her area.
2. For Ben to stop hitting his sister within one week.

Other agreements (or ground rules)

1. For the worker to visit twice a week for the next month on Tuesday and Thursday mornings.
2. For the worker to ring before she visits so Melinda knows when to expect her.
3. For Melinda to be available for all visits.
4. For the two children to be home at least every second visit (on Thursdays).

There is often confusion about what is a task or strategy or solution and what is a goal. Certainly different writers have different definitions of goals and tasks. In simple terms a goal is what the client wishes to achieve, and a task or strategy or solution is a means of achieving it. Finding new accommodation is a goal, whereas looking in the paper and visiting the department of housing are tasks to achieve that goal.

There are as many tasks available to workers as there are problems. William Reid (1985), in his work on family problem solving, refers to session tasks—those carried out within the interview setting; home tasks—those carried out by the clients between sessions; and environmental tasks—which involve liaison with other agencies such as schools or courts. Environmental tasks may be carried out by the worker, the client, other professionals or others within the client's family or social networks.

Once a goal has been identified it is simply a matter of discussing with the client what can be done to achieve that goal.

It is again important that the tasks, strategies or solutions developed to achieve the goals are developed by the client or at least agreed to by the client.

In developing tasks, some discussion may take place about what has been tried previously and there may be some overlap with the problem exploration stage. To some extent this overlap is unavoidable. The important thing is that the client and worker are clear about the nature of the problem and what the client hopes to achieve, and that methods to achieve this are developed.

Tasks, like goals, should be specific and clear. It should be a simple matter to identify whether or not a task has been carried out.

A range of tasks might be carried out within an interview setting. In relation to the goal of employment, tasks might include doing role plays of interviews; working through the newspapers with a client looking for suitable work; discussing with the client different types of work and how suitable they might be; or examining the reasons why previous jobs have not been satisfactory.

Taking an example from probation, a client may be concerned about meeting her unpaid community work commitments; she might therefore identify a goal of getting through the community work hours. Tasks undertaken in the interview might include the worker and client discussing transport arrangements, considering possible alternative community work placements and examining the work commitments of the client.

Taking a situation in child protection where a parent is having difficulty with a child who has temper tantrums, a worker might help the client to identify the circumstances in which the temper tantrums occur. A task to be undertaken within sessions might be to help the mother or father identify what factors might be bringing on the temper tantrums and how these factors could be modified.

Tasks carried out between sessions could include a young person going through the newspaper looking for possible jobs, or a parent trying out strategies to modify the circumstances which lead to a child's temper tantrums. They could involve getting information from the public transport authority about routes and timetables, or getting information about drug rehabilitation centres. They could include a parent taking a child out for a particular activity, or an adolescent ringing up her mother.

Tasks or strategies which might be carried out by the worker include tasks involving advocacy on behalf of a client. This might entail the worker approaching schools, social security, courts or other organisations on behalf of the client. Or it might involve helping the client to write letters to those organisations.

Tasks might also include referral to other agencies, for example, for clients to attend ongoing courses or treatment groups—an anger management course, a sex offenders' group, a women's group, a families first program, a parenting skills course, or a drug treatment program. Such tasks might include shorter-term referrals, such as the client visiting social security, visiting a housing worker, visiting an employment service or making an appointment to see a financial counsellor. In fact, referral to other agencies for particular services is more and more common in work with involuntary clients, as the principles of case management become more prevalent.

Referrals
Making referrals is an important part of work with involuntary clients. It was argued in Chapter 2 that the referral process can be a key factor in achieving positive outcomes for clients. Outlined below are some general principles which can be applied when making referrals.

The referral should, wherever possible, be a part of the problem-solving process. In other words, it should follow the problem survey, problem ranking, problem exploration and goal setting. The referral should preferably be suggested by the client or at least agreed to by the client.

The client should make the initial contact where this is appropriate. There is a good argument for encouraging the client to take as much responsibility as possible for all aspects of the problem-solving process. This is consistent with the idea that clients are learning a process to help solve their own problems, a process which might prove to be useful at a later time.

It may be important, however, that the worker also makes contact with the referral agency. The worker should have information about whether referrals are followed up by clients and whether clients have found the referral helpful. The worker should also be satisfied that the agency provides a service which meets the client's needs.

In making referrals workers should have knowledge about how long the client might have to wait for an appointment. Jack Rothman (1991) points to research which suggests that referrals are more successful if they are followed up by the worker within a few days and the worker actively works together with the referral agency.

In fact, Rothman suggests that in times of dwindling resources and waiting lists, 'case management can be used to project an illusion of responsible care giving . . .' (Rothman 1991:521). Little is likely to be gained by referrals in urgent cases to programs with limited resources and long waiting lists. It may be better in these cases that direct practice workers do some short-term problem solving themselves, even if this can be done over only one or two sessions.

How much a worker should be expected to know about an agency to which referrals are made is a complex issue. Do you simply trust fellow professionals? Or as a worker who supports empirical practice do you examine the nature of the service being offered by other agencies?

One particular dilemma I faced in my work in probation related to referrals to a drug rehabilitation centre. The centre was eventually the subject of a government inquiry into misuse of drugs which had led to the deaths of a number of patients. Prior to this time, however, probation officers had received glossy brochures about the centre's program and many had made referrals to it. It was only subsequently that we thought about the potential risks involved in referring clients to organisations with which we were not familiar.

If programs do not appear to be consistent with the research about what works then referral to those groups is not appropriate. In fact the evidence seems clear that some welfare programs are actually harmful, and it seems hard to justify an approach which simply trusts fellow workers to do the right thing. For example, a probation officer should exercise care in referring a young offender to a 'scared straight' or 'day-in-gaol' program, given the lack of research support for such programs (Lipsey 1991; Gendreau 1996). Unfortunately the welfare field has seen too many programs which do not have an empirical base and are potentially harmful (Trotter 1996b).

Group work
The focus of this book is on direct practice with individual clients and with families. Group work is outside its scope. Nonetheless in developing tasks, workers often refer to group programs and some comment about the use of groups is appropriate.

When is group work appropriate rather than individual work with clients? Allan Brown (1992) reviewed some of the research about the effectiveness of group work and suggests that the state of knowledge is insufficient to say when it is more or less appropriate than individual work.

That said, groups are offered for a wide range of involuntary clients—with some apparent advantages and disadvantages. Groups can provide a source of support to their members, they may be influential in changing attitudes and they may provide a more economical way of dealing with a large client caseload. On the other hand, as discussed in Chapter 2, peer group association which occurs in groups can lead to negative outcomes. There is evidence of this in probation (Trotter 1995a) and to some extent in mental health (Videka Sherman 1988).

It does appear that effective groups are characterised by the same effective practices as outlined in this book (see Ferguson 1983; Videka Sherman 1988; Milgram & Rubin 1992). In making decisions about whether individual or group work is most appropriate, workers should consider the extent to which programs are consistent with the principles of effective practice.

Ongoing review

The point has already been made that the problem-solving process must be used flexibly. The worker and client could be in the middle of developing goals or working through strategies in relation to a particular issue when it becomes evident that another problem should take precedence. It could be that the client has been in denial until that time about a problem or that a new problem emerges. In these cases it may be appropriate to return to the problem survey and problem-ranking stages and effectively start the problem-solving process over again.

Nonetheless, as I have said, the worker should attempt to ensure that the intervention does follow the problem-solving steps as far as possible. It is the responsibility of the worker to provide the structure, to give the client information about how the structure works, and to use the structure flexibly. As suggested earlier, having the structure displayed for clients to see can facilitate this (see Appendix).

The worker and client should regularly review how they are going in relation to the model as a whole and to the individual steps. A regular review of identification of problems, performance of tasks and movement toward goals should take place. This can be linked with ongoing evaluation as discussed in Chapter 8.

PROBLEM SOLVING, ASSESSMENT AND CASE PLANNING

Workers with involuntary clients often have a dual purpose: to investigate and gather information about their clients for official decision-making purposes, and to help those clients with their problems. How does the problem-solving process relate to the assessment and case planning processes?

Assessment and investigation

As indicated above, the problem survey ideally begins in the first interview following some discussion about the role of the worker. The nature of the first interview varies according to the particular setting. In child protection, workers often have their first contact following an allegation of child abuse. The worker generally visits the family in their home in order to investigate the allegations and offer assistance. First contacts in probation sometimes occur at court either before or after the client has been sentenced. First contacts in mental health sometimes occur at a hospital or following an after-hours call from police. In a school setting they might occur immediately following an outburst in the classroom.

In other words first contacts often occur at a time of crisis. In these instances the workers will need initially to deal with the crisis at hand. This may involve making some immediate decisions, such as removal of a child or hospitalisation.

In other cases the first contact with a client will be after a court case and sentencing have been completed, after a case of child abuse has been substantiated, or after a mental health patient has been released from hospital. In these instances the worker and client are more likely to have time to work through an assessment process without the pressure of having to make crisis-dictated decisions.

In either case the worker may be asked to work through a specific assessment format which is in use in the particular organisation he works for. Risk assessment frameworks or screening devices are often used in probation (e.g. Andrews & Bonta 1994), child protection (e.g. McPherson et al. 1997) and mental health (e.g. Murdach 1996). Generally these frameworks ask the worker to work through a number of areas of the client's life with a view to assessing the client's needs and likelihood of relapse (e.g. further offending, child abuse, or hospitalisation).

In addition to working through the client's problems, in most cases in work with involuntary clients the assessment process will include collecting information from other sources. For example, a probation officer may have information on file such as a police report about the nature of the offence or a victim impact statement. The probation officer may talk to a juvenile offender's parents or schoolteachers as part of the assessment process. He may also talk to previous probation officers or other welfare professionals who have been involved with the probationer.

Assessment formats or frameworks usually address factors such as family situation and supports, employment, drug use, social networks and supports, psychiatric history, housing, financial situation and leisure interests. The assessment frameworks may also include more specific information, for example, about the client's offending history, about previous notifications for child abuse or about the client's experiences of childhood abuse.

It has been emphasised throughout this book that workers should work with the client's view of the problem. The problem survey consists of clients talking about problems as they perceive them. Yet the investigative nature of work with involuntary clients often involves the worker collecting information and defining problems for the purposes of making decisions about clients' lives.

Chapter 3 discussed the complexity of the worker's dual social control/helping role. As emphasised there, workers should talk to clients about their role and should be specific about the purpose of the intervention. The purpose of gathering information should be clear to the client. Is it being gathered as part of a problem-solving process or is it being gathered for the purposes of making decisions about the client (e.g. revocation of a probation order, removal of a child, hospitalisation or expulsion from school)? Or is it a combination of these things?

If the worker has a dual purpose at the problem-survey stage, to investigate and to help the client with problems, it might be appropriate to work with two problem lists—one a problem list developed through the problem-survey process described above, and the other a list of problems as defined by the worker following the gathering of information from a variety of sources. Such an approach allows for the investigatory nature of the work whilst at the same time recognising the importance of working with client definitions of problems if lasting change is to be achieved. This can lead in turn to the definition of negotiable and non-negotiable problems and issues as discussed below.

How does the problem-solving contract relate to a case plan?

In Chapter 1 a distinction was made between problem solving and case planning. Problem solving involves counselling or therapeutic work with clients, whereas case planning involves the development of longer-term plans, often including the use of community resources.

As discussed in Chapter 1 the distinction between case planning and problem solving is often unclear. There is a degree of overlap between them. Case planning is conceptualised in this book as relating to non-negotiable aspects of the direct practice intervention. A case plan can be conceptualised as the 'bottom line', or what the worker or a court requires of the client. (Case management, on the other hand, involves the ongoing oversight and monitoring of the case plan.)

Chapter 1 illustrated these concepts with an example from child protection. The following example explores the concepts further. A child is placed on a court order following an investigation by child protection workers regarding neglect by her parents. A case plan is developed by the worker in consultation with the client, the client's family, other professionals and other workers in the organisation. The case plan is ratified by a formal case-planning meeting.

The case plan involves the child being placed with relatives for a period of three months with a view to further assessment of the parents' situation. As part of the case plan the parents are asked to maintain regular contact with the child, and the worker is to regularly monitor the contact between the parents and the child. A further case-planning meeting is scheduled in three months to decide whether or not the child is to be returned to the parents.

The family may have been consulted about this case plan, however, they may well not agree with it. The parents may believe that the child should be returned to live with them immediately. The case plan is, however, non-negotiable, or at least can only be changed by the worker. It constitutes a set of requirements or expectations within which the problem-solving process may take place.

The worker then oversights or manages the case plan and works through the problem-solving process with the parents (and the child if the child is old enough). The parents might identify having their child returned to them after three months as a goal and the problem-solving process and contract would then focus on this issue. Nonetheless the three-month period during which the child is to be placed away from home is non-negotiable.

Similar examples can be drawn from work with other groups of involuntary clients. In probation a case plan might include non-negotiable areas relating to the court order, such as requirements for completing community work or attending for drug treatment. The problem-solving process and contract might focus on goals relating to employment or becoming drug free.

As discussed in Chapter 3, effective work with involuntary clients involves being clear about what is negotiable and what is not negotiable. The problem-solving process, as it is conceptualised in this book, involves working with issues which are negotiable and being clear about what is negotiable and what is not.

CRITICISMS OF A PROBLEM-SOLVING APPROACH

A number of criticisms have been levelled at problem-solving approaches. Eileen Gambril (1994), for example, provides a general critique of task-centred (or problem-solving) work. Outlined below is my attempt to address some of these criticisms as well as some of the difficulties which workers often experience using the problem-solving framework.

Problem solving is too negative

Problem-solving approaches are sometimes criticised as being negative and focusing on weaknesses rather than strengths. Listing all the things wrong in someone's life and working out which one most needs attention could lead them to a state of despair. A number of writers have pointed to the value of *solution*-focused rather than problem-focused approaches (e.g. DeShazer 1988). They argue that the focus should be on times when things have gone well for the client and on exceptions to the problem rather than the problem itself.

The working model presented in this book, however, focuses very strongly on strengths and successes through the pro-social approach. It focuses on small steps with a high chance of success in the development of tasks, and it includes the purposeful use of an optimistic approach (detailed in Chapter 6).

The assessment process, with its inevitable focus on problems, is a necessary part of work with most involuntary clients. Nonetheless, problem solving, accompanied by the other aspects of the intervention model presented in this book, aims to make the casework experience overall a positive one.

No doubt the strongest argument for accurately defining problems or issues in client terms is the considerable body of research which suggests that such approaches are related to improved outcomes for involuntary clients (Andrews et al. 1979; Reid & Hanrahan 1981; Rubin 1985; Sheldon 1987; Videka Sherman 1988; Jones & Alcabes 1993; Trotter 1996a; Reid 1997b).

What if clients say they have no problems?

How do you use a problem-solving framework when clients insist that they have no problems? In child protection, for example, a parent or an adolescent might say that everything is fine, the situation has been misinterpreted or misjudged and there is no need to do any work with them. Probationers similarly will sometimes express the view that they accept the need to report as required but that they do not want assistance with any issues.

In work with involuntary clients the client has a choice to accept or refuse the helping or counselling services offered to them. Clients can be legally required to receive some services, however they cannot be forced to work through a problem-solving process in any meaningful way. Jones and Alcabes (1993) argue that clients do not become clients until they reach agreement with the worker about the goals of the intervention. Prior to this time, they argue, the worker is simply working toward helping the client to become a client—in other words, toward encouraging the client to accept the offer of helping services.

If clients choose not to identify issues to work on, then the worker has little choice but to focus on issues of role clarification, to make use of the principles of the pro-social approach and relationship skills, and to hope that the client will choose to make use of more therapeutic services at a later time.

The worker might continue to explain to the client that he would like to help work on issues of concern to her, that this has been very helpful with other clients, and that this is part of his job. The worker might offer to work on non-threatening issues with the client—income security benefit, for example. In the long run, however, working through a problem-solving process requires the client to invest some level of trust in the worker. This trust can take time to develop, and might in fact never develop, at least with that particular worker.

Problem solving does not focus on the real problem

It is sometimes argued that problem-solving approaches do not focus on the 'real' problem because of the focus on the problem as the client defines it. Critics taking this line argue that clients often do not understand, or even acknowledge, their own problems. For example, a client may have perpetrated sexual abuse against a child and continue to believe that the child was not harmed by the incident and that he did nothing wrong. Working with the client's definition of the problem may have the worker and the client working toward improving the client's housing or marital relationship rather than focusing on the real problem—that of sexual abuse.

In such instances the worker should encourage the client to identify the real problems as problems. The worker might say to the client, 'It seems to me that your sexual interest in young children has got you into all sorts of trouble in the past. I think we should include this on the list'. However, if the client continues to be unwilling to accept that this is a problem for him then it should not be included in the problem survey. The worker might raise the issue again in subsequent interviews, however until the client agrees it should not be included on the list.

It is important to remember that whilst the worker is working with the client to develop a list of client problems, the worker does not ignore problems which the worker sees but the client doesn't. Through the pro-social approach, the worker should simultaneously encourage the pro-social actions and behaviours of the client, challenge rationalisations and encourage the client to look at problems from different perspectives. There may also be non-negotiable requirements which the client must fulfil that address the 'real' problem. For example the client might be required to seek treatment for sexual problems or not to mix with young people.

Reference was made earlier to the idea of developing two problem lists, one a list of client problems and the other a list of problems as they are perceived by the worker. Some participants in my workshops have found this useful in situations where there is disagreement between the worker and client as to what are relevant problems. It is important, as suggested in Chapter 4, that the worker is explicit about the things that he wishes to change in the client, and lists of problems for both worker and client can be an appropriate method of doing this.

Whilst the worker may aim to encourage the client to recognise the 'real' problem, or may work with two problem lists, it remains crucial that the problems which are subsequently dealt with are viewed by the client as problems. The problem-solving process involves working with problems as the client perceives them.

The collaborative problem-solving model accompanied by the pro-social approach, a focus on role clarification and appropriate use of the relationship, was effective with high-risk probationers in my study, many of whom were in a state of denial (Trotter 1996a). Despite the apparent difficulties, it appears to be the most appropriate way of working with involuntary clients. A more directive approach, which defines the problem and sets tasks for, rather than with the client, is less likely to be successful (see Chapter 2).

What about clients who don't follow through as arranged?

Involuntary clients will sometimes work through the problem-solving process in the interview situation and agree to undertake tasks between interviews, however, when they return for the next interview they will not have done so.

In these circumstances the worker should discuss with the client why the task has not been performed. Was the task actually agreed to by the client? Was the task developed by the worker, the client agreeing only reluctantly? Was the task too difficult? Did the task lack meaning for the client? Was the problem relating to the task not a priority for the client or has it changed in some way? Were obstacles to carrying out the task not identified prior to the task being set?

It is important that failure to perform tasks is not viewed as a failure on the part of the client. A task which is not performed is an unsatisfactory task and needs to be revised.

William Reid (1997b), in a review of research on task-centred practice, points to the importance of preparing clients to undertake tasks. He suggests that tasks are more likely to be completed if clients are offered incentives to complete the task, if potential obstacles are examined and if the task is rehearsed. As discussed earlier, simply assigning a task as a directive is less likely to lead to its successful completion.

How can you use a problem-solving process with intellectually disabled, psychiatrically ill or drug-addicted clients?

The research cited in Chapter 2 with mentally ill, intellectually disabled and drug-addicted clients (e.g. Rubin 1985; Videka Sherman 1988), suggests that working with client definitions of problems and client goals is important to positive outcomes with these groups of clients. Nonetheless, the practical experience of workers is often that it is very difficult to work through a problem-solving process with clients who cannot remember week to week, or day to day, what has been decided—or who consistently misinterpret or misunderstand the worker's meaning.

In these circumstances it seems that the best method is simply to persevere. Whilst it may be appropriate to be directive in relation to the legal requirements of a court order, there is little value in directing clients to perform tasks as part of a problem-solving process. Such an approach is unlikely to be successful in terms of improving client outcomes. Despite the real difficulties which workers experience working collaboratively with this client group, a willingness to persevere with a collaborative approach is likely to be of long-term benefit to the client (Rubin 1985; Videka Sherman 1988).

A case example illustrates this point. A schizophrenic client had a long history of involuntary psychiatric hospital admissions relating to her consistent failure to take her prescribed medication. She would be released from hospital and usually readmitted within about three months. This usually occurred after having been picked up by the police because she was wandering on a busy road, walking around late at night with few clothes on, or for some other potentially self-destructive behaviour.

In working through the problem-solving process with this client following her discharge from hospital, it became apparent to the worker that the client did not see not taking her medication as a problem. She said in fact that she did not like to take the medication because it meant that the voices would go away and she would be lonely. She in fact felt happier without the medication.

The client did, however, define her frequent hospital admissions as a problem. The worker and the client then began to work on the problem as the client defined it, which led in turn to the development of strategies relating to the client's personal safety rather than focusing on her medication.

Problem solving supports the status quo

One further criticism of problem solving is that it supports the status quo. In other words, it focuses on problems as defined by the client which may not take into account broader perspectives. For example, in work with a male perpetrator of domestic violence the client definition of the problem is unlikely to incorporate broader issues of patriarchy and sexism.

Again, whilst the problem-solving approach may have a limited focus, in combination with the pro-social approach there is scope to encourage the client to see things from a different perspective. Using the domestic violence example, the worker may use the pro-social approach to encourage and reward any comments which recognise the difficulties which women experience. The worker may confront sexist comments or patriarchal assumptions on the part of the client. Further, feminist consciousness raising might be used as a task or strategy to address a defined problem.

Critics who argue that problem solving supports the status quo also point to its focus on individuals rather than systems. They suggest that system change rather than individual change is more likely to lead to long-term improvement in problems of child abuse, crime, homelessness and violence. In response to this argument, I would say that direct work takes place with large numbers of involuntary clients around the world. The United States has millions of people in the criminal justice system alone. This is not to say that direct action to change political, social and economic systems is not of vital importance to this particular client group. It is simply to say that direct practice has an important place in welfare and corrections systems around the world. It is important that this work is done well.

CASE EXAMPLE

In this case example a mother, Roslyn, has been leaving her two children aged three and five at home alone, sometimes for several hours. It is a similar situation to that described in the child protection case study in Chapter 3. This is the second visit by a child protection worker to the woman's home. The worker is beginning to work through the problem-survey stage of the problem-solving process.

This interview is carried out by the child protection worker, but had the worker chosen to refer the family to a community agency, a similar interview might have been conducted by a worker from that agency.

Worker: Hi, Roslyn.

Roslyn: Hi.

Worker: How are you?

Roslyn: Oh, not bad, not bad.

Worker: I was saying last week that we could look at some of the issues that are worrying you at the moment. We could work through them and see if there is anything you can do or I can do, or we can do together, to help with these problems.

Roslyn: I've been thinking a bit about that. It is a bit of a worry with the kids. I need some time to myself, I need to be able to go out. There's some things you can't do with kids around.

Worker: I am going to start writing these things down—so I get a list of the issues. The first thing we could put on the list is about the kids.

Roslyn: I need to be able to get out sometimes without the kids.

Worker: So will I write down getting out without the kids?

Roslyn: Yes. I mean I'd like to be able to go out on a Saturday night sometimes, to get a bit of a social life. Maybe go shopping sometimes without the kids, so I don't have to put up with them running riot in the supermarket and embarrassing me.

Worker: They embarrass you?

Roslyn: Yes. Last week Tom knocked a bottle off the shelf and it smashed all over the floor, and he was running all over the place. That's why I don't take them shopping with me, that's why I leave them at home.

Worker: We have talked about that, about leaving them at home, haven't we? And as I mentioned before, this is something that the department is not happy about—I am not happy about it either. However, I can see the problem that you've got with taking them to the supermarket. I know what kids can be like in supermarkets.

Roslyn: Yes, they are terrible.

Worker: So doing the shopping with the kids, that is a problem. You need either to be able to do it without the kids or manage to keep them under control when they are with you. [Showing the notes to the client] I have written down the problem of you getting out, having some independence and also the problem with taking Tom to the supermarket.

Roslyn: Yes, it's two things. Getting out and having some independence, having some time to myself. But, it would be nice if I could take Tom somewhere where he didn't go wild, where he didn't just run all over the place like that. He is often like that at home as well. He just doesn't respect me—just like his father.

Worker: Can you tell me about his father? Does he ever see the children?

Roslyn: He left three years ago, after Tom was born, and I have not seen him since. I have no idea where he is.

Worker: And you have had to raise the children on your own?

Roslyn: Yes.

Worker: It seems very unfair. So tell me more about Tom's behaviour. Does he have a bad temper?

Roslyn: Oh, well he has got a temper but the problem is that he is just out of control. I say 'No' and he just doesn't listen.

Worker: So he doesn't take any notice of you? He won't do what you're telling him?

Roslyn: No. I can tell him to be quiet, not to run around but off he goes and it's like I have not spoken.

Worker: How does he get on with his sister?

Roslyn: They fight all the time. You know, she's playing quietly with something and then along he comes and starts interfering and then she's screaming and hitting him and it gets so frustrating.

Worker: Does he hurt her?

Roslyn: Not yet, but as he gets bigger I think he might. Now it's really just annoying.

Worker: It must be frustrating.

Roslyn: I don't feel like having anyone to the house. If I did make some new friends I wouldn't want to bring them home with the kids running riot like that.

Worker: You would also like to be able to have people at home sometimes without the kids performing? Is that something else we could add to this list?

Roslyn: Yes. I need to be able to get out a bit or have people over or something.

Worker: I'm not saying that I can solve these problems for you, however if we sort out just what is worrying you, there may be something you can do or I can do, or that we can do together, to help the situation. This is the idea of my job. Obviously, you know, I have an issue with the kids being left. You know that, and I've explained that.

Roslyn: Yeah, I know, you told me last time. I know, I know, I can't do it or else we could have to go to court.

Worker: I am pleased to hear you say that. It sounds like you understand the situation. Anyway it seems to me that the best way to ensure that the kids are not left at home is to deal with these other problems that you have got. So that is what I'm hoping to do.

Roslyn: Well, it sort of fixes both problems doesn't it?

Worker: I hope so. What I would like to do is try to get a picture of all of the issues which are of concern to you and then pick one or two of them for a start and see what we can do about them.

Roslyn: OK.

Worker: I have used this method a lot before and also there's a lot written about this way of working. I have found that it is a very good way of working with people which actually gets you somewhere.

Roslyn: Well, it's better than someone just coming in and saying you have to do this and you are doing that wrong.

Worker: You seem to understand what I am saying. Your cooperation in this process is very helpful. I think it will help you and the children too.

Roslyn: Good. I hope so.

Worker: We were talking about these fights that they have. You were saying you get frustrated.

Roslyn: Oh yes. They will be watching TV and I'm trying to get dinner and Mandy starts doing something from school and Tom tries to get all over it. He pulls her

pencils away and throws things around and she just gets
really frustrated and then she gets mad with him. And he is
tough. I mean he is only three but he is really strong for
his age already. He hasn't hurt her yet but he will.
Worker: What have you tried to do about it?
Roslyn: Oh, I yell at them. I yell at them all the time. I
smack them. I tell them not to do it. What more can I do?
But it makes no difference.
Worker: Well, that sounds very irritating, frustrating.

In this example the worker is attempting to get a written list of
the issues which are of concern to Roslyn. Several issues are
identified: getting out without the children; Tom's uncontrollable
behaviour; the fighting between the two children; and not being
able to invite anyone to the house. The worker makes use of the
pro-social principles in emphasising the importance of not leaving
the children unsupervised and in praising the client for her cooperation. The worker also talks about his role. (Whilst role has
been discussed in a previous interview the research referred to in
Chapters 2 and 3 suggests that discussions about role should be
ongoing and frequent.)

This example illustrates a small part of the problem survey.
Once the worker is satisfied that the client has identified the major
issues of concern, the worker and client will move on to the next
stage of the problem-solving process, problem ranking.

SUMMARY

The problem-solving process involves seven steps: (1) problem
survey; (2) problem ranking; (3) problem exploration; (4) setting
goals; (5) developing a contract; (6) developing strategies and tasks;
(7) ongoing review and monitoring. The steps are used flexibly
and the focus is on client definition of problems and goals rather
than worker definitions. The steps are used simultaneously with
the pro-social approach and role clarification and in the context of
an appropriate casework relationship.

Criticisms and questions sometimes expressed about the
problem-solving approach to casework include the following: problem
solving is too negative; the client may say that they have no
problems; the client may fail to follow through on tasks and
strategies; some clients, particularly those with intellectual disability,

drug addiction or psychiatric illness, may have difficulty participating in the process; the process may not address the real problem; and it promotes the status quo by working with individuals rather than systems. Each of these difficulties and criticisms has been addressed, however I also stressed that it is important to persist with the problem-solving approach, along with role clarification, and pro-social modelling and reinforcement, if successful outcomes are to be achieved. The client–worker relationship may also be an important factor and this is discussed in the next chapter.

6 | The relationship

CHAPTER 2 HIGHLIGHTED different aspects of the 'casework relationship' including empathy, optimism, humour and self-disclosure. Some social work and welfare texts include other factors in discussions about the casework relationship, for example, the use of authority, confidentiality and genuineness. The focus on work with involuntary clients has led me to place discussion about these factors in other sections of the book. The use of authority is discussed as part of role clarification in Chapter 3 and as part of the pro-social approach in Chapter 4. The issue of confidentiality is discussed under role clarification in Chapter 3. Similarly, the issue of genuineness or being open is discussed in Chapters 3 and 4.

This chapter discusses empathy, optimism, humour and self-disclosure. It also includes a discussion about worker safety and dealing with violent clients.

EMPATHY

Empathy is defined by Hogan (1969:307) as 'the intellectual or imaginative apprehension of another's condition or state of mind'. It involves a 'willingness to put oneself in another's place'. Empathy can be measured by the use of an empathy test or scale (see Trotter 1990).

Reflective listening is a practical manifestation of empathy. It involves a worker responding in an understanding manner to comments made by the client. It recognises both the feeling and content of the client's expressions. It also involves the worker physically attending to the client, making eye contact, for example.

Andrews et al. (1979) found a positive correlation between the scores of probation officers on a scale of empathy and those officers' use of reflective listening practices. In other words, empathic people tend to make use of reflective listening practices, and those making use of reflective listening practices tend to be empathic.

Chapter 2 pointed to research which suggests that in work with involuntary clients there is no clear relationship between worker effectiveness and scores on empathy scales or use of reflective listening practices. In other words, more empathic workers seem to do no better with their clients than less empathic workers.

On the other hand, there is some evidence (cited in Chapter 2) that empathy skills are valuable if accompanied by the use of other effective practice skills, such as the use of a pro-social approach, problem solving and appropriate role clarification. Certainly the collaborative practice model promoted in this book assumes that workers have a capacity to understand the client's point of view. It is appropriate therefore to consider the nature of empathy and reflective listening and how these skills can be integrated with other effective approaches.

What are reflective or empathic listening practices? Reflective listening involves paraphrasing the statements of another person. Robert Carkhuff (1969) developed scales for assessment of interpersonal functioning which included a scale of empathic understanding. At level 1, the worker communicates no awareness of the client's feelings or expressions—in other words, is uninterested or operating from a 'pre-conceived frame of reference'. At level 5, the worker's responses 'add significantly to the feeling and meaning of the expressions' of the client (Carkhuff 1969:317). The worker is 'tuned in' to the client.

The following sets out an example of a low-level empathic response (worker 1), a medium-level empathic response (worker 2) and a high-level empathic response (worker 3).

> *Client:*   I am sick of this. I have no money. I can't pay the rent and I need a job. But there aren't any jobs anywhere. I am going to have to do something.
> *Worker 1:*   Don't worry. It's the same for everyone at the moment.
> *Worker 2:*   You just feel that everything is hopeless.
> *Worker 3:*   You sound like you are feeling pretty desperate. Lack of work and money are real problems.

The third comment responds to the client's feelings and to the meaning or content of the client's expressions.

In work with involuntary clients the worker might make use of the pro-social approach and role clarification in response to this comment. If, for example, the client were a probationer who has a history of property offences the conversation might go something like this:

> *Client:* I am sick of this. I have no money. I can't pay the rent and I need a job. But there aren't any jobs anywhere. I am going to have to do something.
> *Worker:* You sound like you are feeling pretty desperate. Lack of work and money are real problems. I am pleased that you have decided to tell me about this. I would like to help you sort things out if I can.

The worker is offering a verbal reward to the client for having raised the problem, a problem which is likely to relate to his offending behaviour. The worker is also making it clear that she perceives her role as helping the client with problems such as these.

The differences between the empathic response alone and the response which incorporates empathy, role clarification and pro-social reinforcement seem minimal. It does appear, however, as discussed in Chapter 2, that in work with involuntary clients the use of empathic comments alone in these situations can be unhelpful—particularly in response to client expressions which might be justifying or rationalising anti-social or criminal behaviour.

The following example from child protection involves a mother who has hit her two-year-old twins resulting in them being admitted to hospital. The family is subsequently placed on a supervision order.

> *Mother:* The children are so naughty at the moment. I put them to bed for their afternoon sleep and they just lie there and scream. They drive me mad.

An empathic response might be:

> *Worker:* You seem to be very frustrated. Kids are such hard work aren't they?

A response which incorporated the principles of effective work with involuntary clients might be:

> *Worker:* You sound very frustrated. I am pleased that you

can talk to me about these feelings. I would really like to help you sort out some other ways of dealing with the kids. Was this how you felt when you hit the children last month?

This response acknowledges the client's feelings, it reinforces the fact that the client is talking about her feelings, it refers to the helping role of the worker, and it makes it clear that the worker believes alternatives need to be found for the anti-social behaviour of the client.

To respond to every comment by a client with responses which include each of the principles of effective work with involuntary clients is both impractical and undesirable. It is, however, important that the worker responds in a genuine manner and that the effective practice skills become part of the worker's natural style. These examples simply illustrate the skills which in practice might be used over a longer period.

Touching

One issue which is sometimes raised by workers with involuntary clients, particularly those who work in residential settings, is the extent to which it is appropriate to use physical expressions of warmth toward clients.

Workers sometimes touch or hug clients at times of stress for those clients. Certainly touch can be a powerful method of communicating feelings. Some workers say that it is important in the development of their relationships with clients and that they feel comfortable with it. It could be argued that appropriate physical contact with clients is part of pro-social modelling. Unfortunately knowledge about the relative advantages and disadvantages of physical contact is very limited. It is a topic rarely addressed in the welfare literature.

Given this limited knowledge it is not possible to offer any prescriptive guidelines. It is clear, however, that physical contact can be offensive, and male workers in particular should exercise great care in the use of physical contact with clients. When physical contact is part of the client–worker relationship it should relate to the specific role the worker plays with the client. For example, some level of physical contact may be appropriate for residential workers who fulfil fulltime carer roles, but is not likely to be appropriate for probation officers in the normal course of their duties.

OPTIMISM

It was argued in Chapter 2 that workers who are optimistic are more likely to help their clients—that worker optimism is one factor, among others, which relates to positive client outcomes. The concepts of 'hope' (that if workers are hopeful about their clients' prospects their clients are likely to do better) and self-efficacy (that if clients expect to do well they are more likely to do so) were also referred to.

An optimistic approach by workers is consistent with and facilitates the use of other skills by workers. For example, in using the pro-social approach the worker focuses on the client's strengths and rewards positive comments and actions. In problem solving the worker aims for short-term successes in relation to achievable goals.

Involuntary clients, however, on the whole have little reason to feel optimistic. They have been judged by the community as being deviant in one way or another and have been sanctioned by the community for this deviance. They are likely to feel stigmatised and in many cases pessimistic about the future. On top of this (as discussed in Chapter 2) workers are often pessimistic about prospects for their clients.

Yet in this context it is important that workers foster hope and optimism. How can workers be optimistic? What does this mean in day-to-day practice with involuntary clients?

Workers should believe in their capacity to help. A worker who is clear about the theoretical basis of her work and who is familiar with research about the effectiveness of the approaches she is using can communicate to the client her confidence in her ability to help—or at least her confidence that she can help the client to help himself.

The worker might say to the client: 'I have made use of this approach with my clients in the past and they have found it very helpful. I think you will also find it helpful.' Or: 'I think I can help you sort out some of these problems.'

When clients present pessimistic interpretations of events these should be challenged. Martin Seligman (1995) reports on the success of programs with depressed schoolchildren which taught them to challenge pessimistic interpretations of events. Similarly, solution-focused approaches (e.g. DeJong & Miller 1996) emphasise the importance of focusing on successes or exceptions in counselling work. Their proponents argue that the worker should focus on when things went well rather than when things went badly.

The following is an example of a positive interpretation of a client comment. The client says: 'My mother is a very bad-tempered woman and impossible to live with.' The worker responds: 'Do you mean that your mother was in a bad temper this morning? I thought you had been living with her for many years. Are there occasions when she is not in a bad temper?'

Or a client might comment: 'I could not go back to school. I failed everything when I was there.' This might attract a response from the worker such as: 'I understand from your school report on the file that you passed one subject in the last year at school but that you did little work. It seems to me that you might well have the ability to do well at school.'

The use of optimism can also help clients to see their situation in its social and political context. Take, for example, a single mother with four children who feels that she will never be able to give her children the things they should have. The worker might try to help the woman understand that she is not to blame for her situation, that there are many women in a similar position to her and that she can still be a good mother despite her disadvantages.

Pessimistic thinking might be identified as a problem for a client through the problem-solving process. The worker might then be able to help the client work through strategies for dealing with negative thinking. Martin Seligman (1990, 1995) outlines a number of strategies developed from his research in this area—including learning to argue with your own pessimistic thinking; looking for alternative explanations; and learning that thoughts are at least to some extent within the control of the thinker.

Similarly, a client's difficulties in accepting praise and accepting their capacity to do things well could become a target in the problem-solving process. This might initially be a problem identified by the worker but come to be one which the client recognises as well. Strategies for it might involve asking clients to identify things that they like about themselves. The use of products such as strengths cards developed by an Australian Family Care agency to help clients identify their strengths, could be useful for this purpose (Scott & O'Neill 1996). Similarly, workers might help clients to identify their hopes for the future or to respond appropriately to the worker's positive comments.

In attempting to be optimistic, workers should be careful not to overdo it. Furstenberg and Rounds (1995), in their review of self-efficacy in social work, suggest that workers are more likely to be persuasive with clients if they are viewed as credible. The client must believe that the worker understands the nature of the client's world. In other words, optimism which recognises difficulties, rather than optimism which trivialises those difficulties, is more likely to be persuasive.

Finally, it is important that optimism is not confused with the notion of minimisation in work with involuntary clients. It is important that the worker believes in the capacity of the client to change. However, as emphasised in the pro-social approach, it is also important that the worker in no way minimises the anti-social behaviour which has led the client to become a client.

HUMOUR

It was pointed out in Chapter 2 that the use of humour by workers may be related to client outcomes. It seems that there are appropriate and inappropriate ways to use humour.

The literature on use of humour with involuntary clients is limited. There is, however, some literature on its use in welfare settings. Max Siporin, in an article entitled 'Have you heard the one about social work humour?', argues on the basis of several research studies that humour can 'provide an emotionally arousing dynamic for confronting, provocative insight giving and empathic helping procedures' (Siporin 1984:461). He goes on to suggest that humour can be used to help clients deal with and distance themselves from problems and defuse anger.

David Pollio argues in favour of the therapeutic benefits of humour in crisis intervention settings. He suggests that 'positive outcomes of humour include breaking an impasse in the therapeutic process, reframing the context of the problem situation, freeing and empowering the client system and humanising the situation' (Pollio 1995:378). He suggests that negative uses of humour include humour in which the client misinterprets the situation, humour which demeans the client or leaves the client confused.

Humour can be used in situations of extreme emotion which the worker and the client find difficult to handle. There are instances when it is important for both worker and client to maintain sufficient composure to work through the problem-solving process and some use of humour might enable them to do this. For example, a client discussing the recent death of a loved one might be encouraged to talk about some of the lighter moments of that person's life, leading to some laughter between worker and client.

Some guidelines on humour which might be useful to workers with involuntary clients are outlined below. These are developed from my reading of the literature, from comments made by professional workers in my workshops and from work done in an unpublished paper by Jennifer Armstrong (1994) on the role of humour. It should be re-emphasised that the research in this area is limited and the following guidelines are suggestions rather than developed principles of practice.

Constructive humour

Humour which is likely to have positive outcomes includes humour which comes naturally to the situation and which is not contrived; humour which gives the client the sense that they are being treated as a person rather than merely as a client; humour which lightens an overly tense interview situation; humour which responds directly to the client's comments or which picks up on light or humorous comments by clients; and humour which acknowledges the client's feelings in a non-threatening way.

Some examples of humour which professional workers with involuntary clients have found constructive include the following:

- A female child protection worker has made many visits to a family, and whilst the worker has a good working relationship with the mother, the mother's partner has been very angry toward the worker, although in recent visits he has been more reasonable. When she visits she is greeted by both parents at the door and the mother says: 'It is nice to see you.' The father mumbles something which also sounds like: 'It is nice to see you.' The worker says to the father: 'I am not hoping for "nice to see you" but we are progressing aren't we?' All three laugh and the interview gets off to a good start.

  The humour is used to acknowledge the clients' and the worker's feelings, to reinforce the progress in the relationship between the father and the worker, and to relieve the tension between them.

- A woman who had been abused and placed in state care as a child now faces a similar situation with her oldest child being placed in foster care. In a long and tense interview with the foster care worker the mother is talking about her contact with welfare agencies over the years. The worker comments: 'You must have seen about 50 different social workers over the past twenty years.'

The client responds: 'It's more than that and not many of them have helped me.' The worker then says: 'You would think with all those social workers you would not have a problem in the world.'

Both laugh and it relieves some of the tenseness of the situation. Again in this instance the client's experience with so many social workers, and her cynicism about them, is acknowledged but it is done in a way which is not threatening to either worker or client.

Destructive humour

Humour which should be avoided includes: humour which is used to avoid discussions about sensitive topics, for example about personal relationships; humour which is in any way sarcastic or used to put down the client (or anyone else); humour which aims to show how clever the worker is; humour which gives the client the feeling that they are not being taken seriously; and the telling of jokes.

SELF-DISCLOSURE

Self-disclosure has been discussed a lot in literature on counselling and psychotherapy. It is sometimes seen as a manifestation of worker genuineness or authenticity.

Robert Carkhuff (1969), in his work on effective counselling methods, suggests that self-disclosure is one of the key counselling skills. He developed a measure which can be used to rate the extent of self-disclosure by therapists or counsellors in interviews. Low levels of self-disclosure are characterised by the worker actively attempting to remain detached from the client and disclosing 'nothing of his own feelings or personality' (Carkhuff 1969:321). High levels of self-disclosure are characterised by the worker volunteering 'very intimate and often detailed material about his own personality'.

The extent to which self-disclosure is helpful in work with involuntary clients and just how that self-disclosure should be offered is uncertain. The difficulty of disentangling self-disclosure from other relationship factors and the lack of research on self-disclosure in work with involuntary clients contribute to this uncertainty.

Nonetheless, there are a number of guidelines which might be offered to assist workers in making decisions about self-disclosure. These are taken in part from a set of guidelines developed by Anderson and Mandell (1989).

Self-disclosure which involves non-intimate details about a worker's life, such as whether the worker is married or has children, is generally appropriate, particularly in situations where clients are expected to disclose very personal material. This is consistent with research by Shulman (1991) and with the principles of pro-social modelling referred to in Chapter 4.

Self-disclosure is particularly valuable if workers wish clients to disclose personal matters (Anderson & Mandell 1989). It seems that personal comments such as 'I found it very difficult when my children were young' or 'when I was unemployed' or 'after I separated from my partner' will encourage clients to disclose more personal material about themselves.

Self-disclosure, or modelling, which refers to difficulties the worker has experienced is likely to be more helpful than self-disclosure which refers to the worker's achievement (Derlega & Berg 1987). For example, a worker who talks about how she has been able to find work easily in the past is less likely to motivate a client than one who talks about how difficult it was to find work, how she became quite depressed by the situation but was eventually successful.

Self-disclosure should not shift the focus of the interview from the client to the worker. Self-disclosures should be brief and for the purpose of showing empathy for the client's situation. It hardly needs saying that the focus of interviews should be the client's problems rather than those of the worker.

Nor should self-disclosure be too intimate (Anderson & Mandell 1989). A comment that the worker found it very difficult to handle a broken relationship some years ago might be appropriate. A comment that the worker is in a state of depression following a recent marital breakdown is not likely to be appropriate.

Care should be used with clients who are likely to misinterpret self-disclosures. For example, self-disclosure may be inappropriate with some schizophrenic or heavily dependent clients.

Sandra Anderson and Deborah Mandell (1989) also suggest that self-disclosure should be mentioned as part of the role clarification:

it should be pointed out that 'therapist self disclosure is an expected part of treatment'. In other words, the worker should explain that she may refer briefly to her own experiences to help her understand the way the client is feeling.

To summarise: it does seem that some level of self-disclosure in work with involuntary clients is appropriate. Whilst the extent and nature of this self-disclosure is largely dependent on the situation, the fear some workers have about self-disclosure appears to be inappropriate, particularly when this involves a reluctance to disclose even the most minor details whilst at the same time expecting detailed disclosures from clients.

THE AGGRESSIVE CLIENT

Work with involuntary clients often involves working with clients who are both aggressive and violent. A number of studies of client violence in social work settings have suggested that as many as 25 to 30 per cent of social workers have been physically assaulted during their careers (Rey 1996). In her paper, Lucy Rey also refers to studies undertaken with psychiatrists and psychologists who report even higher rates of assault.

An Australian study by Tom Puckett and Helen Cleak (1994) found that 31 per cent of welfare workers had been physically assaulted in their careers, with many more having been abused verbally or threatened. The sample included social workers, welfare workers and youth workers working in a range of settings with predominantly involuntary clients. More than half the assaults took place at the client's residence and, perhaps surprisingly, more than half were in the presence of one or more of the worker's colleagues.

In work with involuntary clients, physical safety is clearly an important issue, and should not be minimised as it was by senior staff in one survey of United States social workers by Lucy Rey (1996). It should, however, be placed in context. Puckett and Cleak (1994) also cite studies, for example, which suggest that more than 90 per cent of clients do not pose any threat to workers.

A number of practical strategies have been suggested which might minimise the likelihood of becoming a victim of client violence (Rey 1996; Puckett & Cleak 1994).

- Workers should attempt to assess the risk that particular clients pose. Christina Newhill (1996), in a survey undertaken with social workers in the United States, found that young men were more likely to be perpetrators of violence and that their victims were most likely to be male workers. Particular care should be exercised when visiting young men in their homes particularly if they have a history of violence, drug abuse or the use of weapons. In these situations enlisting the assistance of the police might be appropriate.

- Interviews in client homes should be conducted in the front of the house so that the worker has access to the door in case she wishes to make a quick exit. If workers feel unsafe they should not enter the client's home.
- Workers should always inform someone from their office where they are going and if possible take a mobile phone.
- Interview rooms in offices should be set up so that the worker has ready access to the door and can leave the room quickly if necessary. A worker who has their desk away from the door leaving the client between herself and the door is vulnerable. An emergency alarm in interview rooms should be standard in work with involuntary clients. Interview rooms should not contain heavy objects. If possible rooms should have two exits.
- If workers feel threatened they should avoid confronting clients, and listen to what the client is saying. If the client has a sense that he is being listened to it may reduce his frustration and his aggression. The worker should then extricate herself from the situation as soon as possible.

For detailed strategies for preventing and dealing with client violence the reader is referred to Braithwaite (1992) and Bowie (1996).

SUMMARY

The relationship is defined in this chapter as including empathy, optimism, humour and self-disclosure. Other texts include other factors in the relationship, such as the use of authority, confidentiality and genuineness. These factors are addressed in other sections of this book.

Empathy—or the ability to understand another's point of view—is a helpful skill in work with involuntary clients when it is accompanied by the other skills of problem solving, a pro-social approach and role clarification. Optimistic workers seem to communicate this optimism to their clients who in turn do better. The worker's use of humour is an unresearched area in work with involuntary clients but it does appear that appropriate use of humour may be related to positive outcomes. Similarly, little work has been done on the use of self-disclosure, however there is some indication that it may contribute towards positive outcomes in work with involuntary clients.

The chapter also considered worker safety.

7 | Working with families

WORK WITH INVOLUNTARY clients often involves working with families. Probation officers may work with the parents and extended family of juvenile offenders, as well as the partners or extended family of adult offenders. Child protection workers work with the families of abused and neglected children. Mental health workers work with family members as do workers in domestic violence, school welfare, and youth work.

In work with involuntary clients whole families may be clients, for example in child protection, when a family might be placed under supervision by a court. Often, however, a single client is involuntary and involvement with the client's family is on a more voluntary basis. For example, a probationer is an involuntary client, but the probationer's partner or mother are not involuntary clients.

The term 'family' is interpreted broadly in this book. Family members may include foster parents or same sex partners for example. Family is defined as any two or more people who live in intimate relationships with each other.

WHEN IS IT APPROPRIATE TO WORK WITH FAMILY GROUPS?

It is possible to work with families on a family group basis or with members individually. Working with a family group usually involves two or more family members working with a family worker through a range of problems or issues which are of concern to the family members.

Work on an individual basis with family members involves the worker seeing the different family members separately. Workers may, for example, work with the family members of a mental health client independently from that client. Workers might spend time educating family members about the nature of the mental illness and the role they might play in supporting the client. This should of course occur with the client's knowledge and as part of a problem-solving process, nonetheless the client may not be directly involved in the work with other family members.

Work with family groups is not the most common form of practice with involuntary clients. In fact Mary Russell (1990) cites a number of studies which suggest that even family therapists are more likely to work with individuals or couples rather than family groups.

Certainly family work of any type is unlikely to be appropriate when a client's problems are clearly individual problems—in situations where there is no apparent link between the client's problems and other family members. Family work is not likely to be appropriate if the client does not live with or interact closely with other family members.

Where family work is appropriate there are occasions when work with individual family members may be more appropriate than work with family groups. Some of these occasions are outlined below.

Work with family groups is generally not appropriate with a perpetrator and victim of sexual or serious physical assault. This is not to say that there are never occasions when work with a perpetrator and a victim is appropriate. For example, a perpetrator who understands the damage that his actions have caused might apologise to the victim for his actions. This could take place in a family counselling session as part of a plan to help a victim deal with issues of guilt. However, generally speaking, family work which makes use of a mediation style, as described later in this chapter, is unlikely to be appropriate in situations where one family member is clearly a victim of sexual or physical assault and another a perpetrator of that assault.

Where it is apparent to the worker that there is a severe power imbalance in the family, family group work is unlikely to be appropriate. For example, a father might be very dominant in the family situation and other family members intimidated by him and afraid to express their ideas in his presence. Individual work might be more appropriate in this instance. The worker might work on these issues with the father with a view to involving the family group at a later stage. In the short term, however, family work as it is described in this chapter, assumes that family members feel free to express their views without fear of retribution.

In situations where the worker has a value clash with certain family members family group work is also likely to be inappropriate. For example, a worker might feel unable to work with parents who will not allow their twenty-year-old daughter to go out with men alone, or with parents who believe in female circumcision. In these instances working individually with the parents and the daughter might be more appropriate.

On the other hand, it was argued in Chapter 2 that there are many instances in work with involuntary clients when it may be more appropriate to work with a family group rather than with individuals. The positive outcomes achieved in some family counselling programs certainly suggest this (e.g. Gordon et al. 1988).

Working with a family group is likely to be appropriate in situations where issues raised by the client are related to family interaction patterns; where family interaction patterns appear to relate to the reason the client is a client (e.g. a young person who offends after being told to leave home); and where increased levels of understanding of each other's point of view is likely to help family interaction.

In situations where individual work is being carried out it may become apparent that family work is the most appropriate method of dealing with a particular problem. For example, if in working through the problem-solving process a probationer identifies problems in his relationship with his partner, a task might be set to work through issues in one or more joint sessions with that partner.

WHY FAMILY PROBLEM SOLVING?

There are many family therapy, family counselling and family mediation models which have been used in work with both voluntary and involuntary clients. Arthur Horne and Laurence Passmore (1991), for example, refer to seventeen different family therapies in their book on family counselling and therapy. Some examples include structural, strategic, gestalt, rational emotive and transactional analysis therapies.

It is not within the scope of this book to examine the range of family therapy models. This chapter outlines one model for working with families—a problem-solving model. The model presented owes much to models developed by Epstein and Bishop (1981), Forgatch and Patterson (1989) and Reid (1985, 1992).

I have chosen to present this particular family work model for several reasons. It is consistent with the general principles of effective practice with involuntary clients outlined in Chapter 2. In fact the model as it is presented attempts to incorporate each of the approaches which the research suggests are related to effective outcomes.

As pointed out in Chapter 2, family problem solving has been used and tested in work with a range of involuntary clients in such settings as child protection, juvenile justice, mental health and youth work (Reid 1985, 1992).

Family problem solving has also been applied and tested with considerable success with a range of both voluntary and involuntary clients in my own research (Trotter 1997b). As mentioned in Chapter 2, 100 per cent of clients in my study, many of whom were involuntary, indicated that they benefited from a family problem-solving intervention offered by students and professionals. The research support for family problem solving is in contrast with the lack of such support for many family therapy approaches (Wynne 1988; Horne & Passmore 1991).

An additional advantage of the problem-solving model is that it can be learned relatively quickly by workers with some professional training and/or experience. My research with both social work students and professional welfare workers (Trotter 1997b) found that these people, even though they had minimal experience in family counselling, were able to successfully carry out a series of family counselling sessions after about sixteen hours of training.

STEPS IN THE FAMILY PROBLEM-SOLVING PROCESS

The family problem-solving model outlined below uses the same steps as the problem-solving model presented in Chapter 5: problem survey; problem ranking; problem exploration; setting goals; developing a contract; strategies and tasks; and review. Like problem solving with individuals the process should be accompanied by appropriate role clarification, pro-social modelling and reinforcement, and appropriate use of the relationship.

The family problem-solving process can be undertaken with two or more family members. Ideally all family members caught in the family dynamics should be involved although the process can still work well if only some members of the family choose to participate. Children should be able to participate in this process if they are old enough to follow the discussion, usually from around ten years of age.

Role clarification

Before the problem-solving process gets under way the worker should discuss the role of the worker and what is expected of family members. In addition to working through the role-related factors outlined in Chapter 3, the worker should also discuss the specific roles of participants in the family problem-solving process. For example, it might be explained at the outset that the worker aims to take a neutral stance—that no one person's point of view will be supported over another's, and that the aim is to reach agreement between family members. It might also be explained that all family members are expected to attend a certain number of sessions. It might further be explained that each family member is to allow other family members to speak uninterrupted, and that participants are expected not to shout or be abusive. And it might be explained that individual family members are free to talk to the worker between sessions on a confidential basis.

Setting ground rules such as these at the outset is likely to facilitate a less volatile process.

The worker should also introduce the family problem-solving model to the client family and explain briefly how it works, particularly its focus on helping the family to solve problems themselves. It might be useful to display the family problem-solving steps in the interview room so that family members can follow the steps of the model as the sessions progress. If the interview is conducted in the family home a piece of paper outlining the steps might be given to family members (see Appendix for an outline of the problem-solving steps).

Pro-social approach

Whilst the worker may be neutral in terms of not favouring particular family members, she should, as in work with individuals, encourage pro-social comments and actions on the part of family members. This includes encouraging and rewarding the ongoing involvement of family members in the family problem-solving process. Family members should be encouraged and rewarded for attending sessions, identifying problems, following through on tasks and generally participating in the process.

Problem survey

The purpose of the family problem survey, like the problem survey with individual clients, is to identify issues which are of concern to family members. The worker asks each family member to describe in turn issues which are of concern to them or things about family relationships which they would like to change. As each person identifies issues or problems the worker writes these down in the person's words, either in file notes or on a white board. It is important that the family members are able to see the list as it is written.

It might be appropriate to ask the less powerful, or forceful, family members to speak first to encourage an equal involvement in the process. It might also be appropriate to specify that each family member has a specific time to talk about their issues, say up to five minutes, to ensure that particular family members do not dominate.

The worker should encourage family members to express problems in non-blaming terms. For example, the worker might reframe problems for the client. A twelve-year-old girl might say that her biggest problem is her fourteen-year-old sister—'She goes out whenever she likes and I have to stay home'. Following some further discussion the girl might be encouraged to reframe her problem as: 'It upsets me that my mother has different rules about what my sister is allowed to do and what I am allowed to do. I feel like she thinks she cannot trust me.'

Care must of course be exercised to ensure that reframing does not involve the worker restating the problem as the worker sees it. As emphasised throughout this book, it is vital that the problem to be worked on is in fact the client's problem.

The worker should prompt family members to identify problems which are likely to be related to the client's status as an involuntary client. For example, the worker might ask a young person who has been truanting from school to talk about whether school presents a problem for her. Or the worker could ask a young person who has been running away from home to identify specific things he does not like about home.

At the problem survey stage, whilst some clarification of issues is appropriate, the worker should encourage each client to be brief. Further discussion of the issues can take place later. In the early stages it is important that other family members don't have to wait too long to get a turn.

It is also appropriate at this stage to reinforce the idea that family members should not interrupt each other. The family members should be informed that they are free to ask for clarification of points but otherwise they should listen to the speaker until he has finished. Achieving this may of course be difficult, but by insisting on this the process is facilitated and the family may begin to learn about how to listen to each other.

After each client has spoken the worker should have a written list of issues which are of concern to that family member. In some cases the concerns will be common to more than one family member. In other cases they will be specific to the individual.

Once each person has spoken and the worker has a list of all the issues, the worker should try to identify the common ones. If none of the problems expressed by the different family members are the same the worker should try to reframe or redefine the problems as common problems. For example, it may be that a mother is concerned about her daughter's truancy. The daughter may not be worried about her truancy but might be distressed about her mother's angry outbursts about her truancy. There is therefore a common concern about school. The common problem is disagreement about school attendance and the problem could be defined in this way.

Or a young person may be concerned that his mother is hardly ever home. In this instance the worker might ask other family members whether this is a problem for them. The worker might ask the mother if she is concerned about the amount of time she is able to spend with her son. It might in this way be possible to define the problem as a common family problem.

Family members may also have problems which are of concern only to themselves and these can sometimes be better dealt with at the individual level. For example, a mother might be unhappy in a relationship and her son may feel this is of no concern to him.

Thus at the completion of the problem survey the worker should have a list of problems for each family member. As far as possible these problems should be defined as common problems, however it may be that some individual problems will remain.

Problem ranking

The aim is then to make a decision about which problem or problems to work on. The worker should keep in mind the guidelines for problem ranking referred to in Chapter 5. The problems to be worked on should be the family's own problems, they should as far as possible be problems that are amenable to change, and for which resources are available, they should be related to the worker's own goals for the family, and they should relate to practical rather than intra-psychic issues.

It is vital to work with the family's problems as the family members define them. The worker might suggest which problems are most appropriate to begin with, however the family must agree that the problems to be worked on are important. If family members have different problems it may be necessary to work simultaneously on one problem for each family member.

Achievable problems should be addressed first. It might be best, for example, to start with a problem about pocket money rather than a problem relating to a parent who is not involved in the counselling and has no interest in the family.

It is also better to deal with problems for which there are resources available to help. For example, if the family has a problem with inadequate housing then it is much easier to deal with this if there is a possibility of getting better housing than if there isn't.

If one family member is subject to some formal mandate or authority it may be appropriate to start with the formal requirements. For example, if a child is to be expelled from school unless certain things occur, or if a young person is required to undertake certain actions as part of a court order, these problems should take precedence.

The problem-solving model focuses on practical issues or problems. As far as possible the focus should be issues such as housing, employment or drug use, rather than intra-psychic issues such as self-esteem, anxiety or depression.

Finally, if the family or any family members are facing some immediate crisis this might need to be dealt with first. For example, if the family is homeless this would probably have to take immediate priority.

Taking these factors into account the worker should encourage the family to agree on the most appropriate family problem to begin work on. If it is not possible to reach agreement on which problem to work on, it may be appropriate to work on more than one problem. It is vital, however, that each family member feels that the problem which is to be worked on is relevant to them.

Problem exploration

Some of the family problem-solving models do not include a problem exploration stage (e.g. Epstein & Bishop 1981), preferring to move directly from problem ranking to setting goals. Others (e.g. Reid 1985) suggest further problem exploration before moving on to setting goals. Some problem exploration will have taken place during the problem survey, nonetheless, in many cases it is likely to be appropriate to gather some more information about the problem before moving on to goals and solutions.

As suggested in Chapter 5 in relation to individual problem solving, the family members should be asked about the history of the problem. When does it occur? How did it begin? What has the family done to address the problem previously? Have these things helped or hindered? What is the client getting out of it? Are there occasions when the problem is not present? What is different on these occasions?

Goal setting

The next step involves setting goals—clear and specific goals which are agreed to by the worker and the clients and are directly related to the problem(s). The goals answer the question: what does the family want to happen?

Examples of goals include:

- For Tony to move out of home within two weeks.
- For Zac and her spouse Mike to make a decision about whether or not Zac should seek inpatient treatment in relation to alcohol addiction.
- For all instances of domestic violence to cease immediately.

The goals should be as specific as possible so that it is clear to the worker and the client at a later date whether or not the goal has been achieved.

Contract

When the family members have reached agreement about what they wish to achieve then a written contract should be developed summarising the problems to be worked on, the goals to be achieved, and any ground rules or expectations the worker or the client might have in relation to the family problem-solving process. Outlined on page 134 is an example of a family problem-solving contract relating to a fifteen-year-old girl, Amy, who has been placed on probation for stealing which occurred when she ran away with her nineteen-year-old boyfriend.

Family problem-solving contract

Problems

1. Amy and Mrs Larkin (Amy's mother) are worried about Amy being unhappy at home and about her wanting to run away from home again.
2. Amy and Mrs Larkin argue constantly and rarely if ever talk in a civil manner to each other.
3. Amy and Mrs Larkin are unable to agree on whether or how often Amy sees her boyfriend.
4. Amy and Mrs Larkin are concerned about school. Amy is concerned because she feels school offers her nothing but is unsure what else to do and Mrs L. is worried that Amy will miss out on opportunities if she does not stay at school.

Goals

1. For Amy to live at home with her mother and brother on an ongoing basis.
2. For Amy and Mrs L. to report to the worker that they talk to each other in a friendly way and listen to each other for at least five minutes on at least two occasions each week. The aim is for this goal to be achieved by week 3.
3. For Amy and Mrs L. to reach agreement on whether Amy should continue to see her boyfriend and if so how often and where she should see him. This goal to be achieved by week 7.
4. For Amy and Mrs L. to make a decision about whether Amy should stay at school or look for some other way of occupying her time. This goal is to be achieved by week 8.

Ground rules for the family counselling sessions

1. Amy and Mrs L. to attend each session or explain to the counsellor and each other why they are unable to attend. Initially ten sessions will be held.
2. Amy, Mrs L. and the counsellor to listen to each other in counselling sessions and not to interrupt each other except to clarify what is being said.
3. Amy or Mrs L. are free to ask for individual sessions with the counsellors if they wish. These sessions will be confidential.
4. No information to be given to any other people about what goes on in the sessions without the permission of Amy and Mrs L.

Strategies/tasks

Strategies or tasks should then be developed by the worker and family members to address the goals. As outlined in Chapter 5 in relation to individual problem solving, strategies or tasks might be carried out inside or outside the family counselling sessions.

The following are examples of tasks which might be carried out during the sessions. These tasks relate particularly to any goal of improved communication, or more specifically, reducing the number of arguments between family members.

Family members could be asked to listen to each other for a specific period of time (e.g. three minutes) and then asked to paraphrase what has been said. The aim of this task is to teach listening skills which should in turn help to reduce the number of arguments.

Another task relating to communication might involve the use of role play. The worker might ask a mother and her daughter to role play a situation in which arguments commonly occur, for example a discussion about a boyfriend. Then rather than arguing as they normally do they could be asked to focus on listening to the other person and paraphrasing what has been said.

Family members can be asked to reverse roles so that the mother takes the daughter's role and vice versa. This could help them to understand what the situation is like from the other person's point of view. This might have a subsequent impact on the arguments.

Another task which is often used in family problem solving involves teaching clients to give each other positive feedback. Family members might be asked to brainstorm all of the things they like, appreciate or admire about each other and these might be listed on a piece of paper or on the board by the worker. In families where a negative pattern of interaction has developed these positive comments can come as a surprise and sometimes lead to positive changes.

Another task which might be carried out in the interview setting involves brainstorming solutions. In relation to the goal of a young person staying at home, family members might be asked to think up anything which might encourage the young person to remain at home. These ideas could then be listed on a board or piece of paper and worked through to see if they could be developed into specific tasks. Tasks developed in this manner might then be carried out during sessions or at home between sessions.

Some examples of tasks or strategies which might be carried out at home include things like engaging in mutually enjoyable activities, or spending a specified time together. Tasks carried out at home might also involve extended family members. For example, the goal may emerge in discussions between family members for a young offender to have more contact with suitable adult role models. It may be that increased contact can be facilitated with an uncle or another relative. It might even be appropriate to involve extended family members in family problem-solving sessions so they can be involved in developing tasks to address issues identified by the family members.

Sometimes simple tasks can be very powerful. One particularly interesting example is drawn from the practice of a worker in one of my research projects. A twelve-year-old boy, Danuka, was placed on probation following a number of serious offences. He committed these offences after running away from home. He ran away from home often, sometimes staying away for days at a time. His parents did not know where he stayed when he was away from home. A brainstorming task was used with this family, in which the mother, father and Danuka all suggested things which might stop Danuka from running away in the future. Danuka said that he would enjoy home more if someone would play chess with him.

A task was subsequently set for Danuka and his father to play chess once per week (subsequently increased to twice per week). The chess playing continued during and after the family's involvement in family counselling and it seemed to be highly influential in Danuka continuing to stay at home. The task seemed to allow for the attention Danuka wanted from his father and their relationship improved dramatically. The offending also stopped.

This seems like such a simple solution to a very complex problem. Its success seemed to lie in the fact that it was a task suggested and designed by Danuka and it addressed what was perhaps Danuka's core problem—his relationship with his father. The problem was addressed in a positive way, the task was easily carried out and it implied no blame or fault on the part of either Danuka or his father.

Review

The final step in the family problem-solving process relates to ongoing monitoring or review. This recognises that it is necessary to continually revise the stages you are at in the problem-solving process. Whilst the steps are straightforward families do not tend to organise their problems with problem-solving processes in mind. The worker should aim to use the problem-solving structure to make sense of the counselling process, however the structure should be used flexibly.

The following case example illustrates this. In this example names and identifying details have been changed, however the example is similar to a case undertaken in the family problem-solving research project referred to earlier (Trotter 1997b).

CASE EXAMPLE

Laura ran away from home at the age of fourteen following a series of arguments with her mother and sister. She stayed with friends for a few days and then approached a youth counselling service for financial assistance. She was subsequently placed in three successive supported accommodation placements over a period of a year, however each placement broke down. The third and final placement broke down due to Laura's extreme introversion, her inappropriate sexual behaviour, her chronic bed-wetting and her violence toward other residents.

She was referred for a psychiatric assessment because of concerns about her bed-wetting and her other problems. The psychiatrist, however, indicated that she had no diagnosable psychiatric illness.

Laura was almost sixteen by this stage and she was told that the agency could no longer provide accommodation for her. Laura's mother, Anne, had expressed a willingness to have Laura return home. It was put to Laura that she would have to return to live with her mother (unless she could work out some other arrangement).

Laura was clear that she did not wish to return home and refused to discuss with workers where she was going to live. At this stage the worker put a proposal to Laura, asking her to attend six family counselling sessions with her mother. It was put to her that if she completed the counselling sessions and still did not wish to return home the worker would do her best to assist her to find alternative accommodation. Laura agreed on this basis. Laura's mother was also agreeable to the arrangement.

Laura was not therefore entirely an involuntary client. At nearly sixteen she could have gone her own way and sorted out her own accommodation and there would have been no legal sanction. On the other hand, she had many personal and interpersonal problems and her placement options were very limited. Whilst she could be defined as partially voluntary, she might be placed more toward the involuntary end of the involuntary–voluntary client continuum, because of her resistance to being involved in the family problem-solving process.

Laura and her mother subsequently attended five family problem-solving sessions with a youth worker at the agency. The mother attended the sixth session alone.

The first family problem-solving meeting was the first time Laura and her mother had met since Laura left home. They had had some phone contact over the past year but had not seen each other during this period. The initial meeting was tense with Laura refusing to look at or speak to her mother. The worker began with a discussion about roles and the nature of the family problem-solving process. Laura and her mother were then asked to identify issues which were concerning them.

Anne talked about the problems leading up to Laura leaving home. She said that she felt that Laura leaving home and refusing to return was an overreaction to the situation. She said that her leaving was precipitated by an argument between Laura and her sister, by Laura's problems at school and Laura's distress about her mother talking to teachers about her. She said Laura also was upset about her mother not allowing her to change schools.

Laura then talked about her problems. She said that she left home only after her mother dragged her outside and threatened to kill her. Laura said she felt and still feels unwanted and that her mother and sister do not care about her opinions. She was unhappy about being told to stay home by her mother as punishment, her mother not talking to her, not liking her friends and her mother talking to schoolteachers behind her back.

Following some discussion Laura stated that she did not wish to discuss going home. Laura and her mother agreed that there was a problem of communication between them. Some tasks were then suggested by the worker, Laura and Anne in relation to a short-term goal of improved communication.

The tasks included:

1. Having a telephone discussion before the next session.
2. Anne to leave the decision about coming home to Laura and not to ask her to come home.
3. Laura not to say that she would never come home.

These tasks were agreed to. At the next session the tasks were reviewed. Anne had rung and they had had a conversation without argument. Laura described it as a 'normal' conversation. No mention was made of Laura coming home. Laura also rang home and spoke to her sister. (She rang for her mother but Anne was not home.)

This was the first contact between Laura and her family (outside the counselling session) for many months, and both Laura and her mother were congratulated by the worker on the successful completion of the task.

The worker then returned to the problem survey and asked Laura and Anne to identify the problems again. They agreed that blaming was a problem and forgiving (or an inability to do so) was a problem. These were problems for both Anne and Laura. There was also a problem with Anne expecting Laura to come home. When Anne mentioned this Laura would get angry and insist that it was not her (Anne's) decision.

Goals were discussed and Laura said that her goal in relation to the problem of forgiving was to not feel angry toward her mother any more. Laura's goal in relation to communication was to talk with her mother more; a goal for both Laura and Anne was not to talk about Laura coming home at this stage. Laura and Anne were able to agree to goals relating to improved communication and forgiving each other.

A number of tasks were suggested by Laura and her mother in relation to the goals of forgiving each other. Laura suggested that her mother apologise for threatening to kill her. Anne was not agreeable to this task. Anne then suggested that Laura go to her family home for afternoon tea next week. All agreed to this. With Anne's encouragement Laura said she would go home after school on Tuesday, Wednesday and Thursday. This was agreed to.

At the next meeting Laura had not carried out the tasks which had been set. She said she did not have time. Laura then said that she hates her mother and her mother hates her. Laura began to talk about how prior to her leaving home more than one year ago, her mother had forced her to go on access visits with her father and how her father had hit her during those visits.

Laura became very emotional and started to cry. She spoke directly to her mother about her feelings. She said that she had explained to her mother at the time that she was scared of her father and she was still forced to go. She felt betrayed by her mother.

The worker allowed this exchange to go for a long period because Anne was listening and Laura was expressing her feelings. As the conversation ensued Anne also started to cry. She said that she had not realised how serious the violence by Laura's father was and how much the visits upset Laura.

This outpouring of emotion and feeling from Laura could be defined as a spontaneously developed task for Laura to talk about her feelings. For the first time her mother listened to and understood Laura's feelings about the abuse perpetrated by her father. It was a powerful moment in the counselling sessions because it was the first time Laura and Anne had seriously discussed this issue.

Toward the end of the session the worker suggested that Laura and Anne hug each other. Laura at first responded 'no way', however it was put to her that this could be viewed as a task which might help both forgiveness and communication. They hugged in a somewhat strained manner. The worker felt that this session task allowed the session to finish on a very positive note.

Immediately after the meeting the worker spoke to Laura and indicated that her time was running out at the supported accommodation placement and that she would have to leave. The worker hoped at this stage that Laura would agree to go home. Laura agreed to 'give it a try'. This marked a dramatic change in Laura who before the family problem-solving sessions had barely spoken to her mother in twelve months. The change seemed to relate directly to the movement toward 'forgiving' her mother following the discussions about the abuse by her father.

The next family session took place three days after Laura returned to live with her family. Laura and Anne were both quite happy with the way things had gone for the three days, however they agreed to keep working on the problems which had been defined in the previous sessions: those of forgiving each other and improved communication with each other.

A task, proposed by the worker, was to be carried out between sessions. The task involved talking to each other for at least ten minutes each day and not raising the past in any blaming way.

The next session occurred one week later. Laura had had an argument with her sister during the week and had hit her. The task of talking had not occurred although there had been no raising of past matters by Laura or her mother.

Laura raised other problems. The worker then returned to the problem survey and added these problems to the issues of forgiveness and communication. Laura said her mother yells at her more than her sister. She also added that she (Laura) is not interested in any long-term relationship with her mother.

Anne was concerned about Laura's swearing and the fact that she had hit her sister.

Two goals were then defined: Laura wanted her mother to yell at her less and Anne wanted Laura to stop swearing.

Tasks were discussed to address these problems. *Quid pro quo* or contingency tasks were agreed to. Laura agreed to stop swearing or at least using 'f' and 'c' words which upset her mother. Anne said she would not yell at Laura.

There was further discussion about the problem of the abuse by the father. Anne talked about how she had been required to facilitate access between Laura and her father and how she had felt powerless to prevent it. Further, she said that she had not realised how serious the violence was. Laura and Anne were again in tears in this discussion. The worker, in encouraging the forgiveness, pointed out to Anne and Laura that Laura's anger should more appropriately be directed toward her father who was the perpetrator of the abuse.

Both Laura and Anne agreed that they needed to forgive each other. The discussion about this issue and Anne's explanation of her thoughts at the time constituted a session task toward the goal of forgiveness.

The session finished with Anne and Laura agreeing to try to carry out the tasks relating to swearing and yelling between this and the next session.

A final visit was scheduled, however only Anne attended the last visit. Anne passed on a message from Laura that she was home now and so she did not have to come. Anne felt that the family problem-solving process had been very helpful primarily because it had helped Laura to decide to return home to live and had helped her (Anne) to better understand her daughter.

A follow-up contact with Anne more than one year later indicated that Laura had remained at home with her mother and sister for one year. Whilst they still had problems they were clearly a family unit. Laura continued at school and satisfactorily completed Year 10. She subsequently moved out of home to live with a friend but was still keeping in contact with her mother and attending school. She continued to have no contact with her father, her clearly expressed wish. Whilst Laura had not wished to raise the issue of bed-wetting in the family counselling sessions, this too had subsided and was no longer a chronic problem.

This case illustrates how the problem–solving structure can be used to facilitate communication between family members even when there are longstanding communication problems. It is likely that Laura would not have returned to live with her mother without this family counselling opportunity.

SUMMARY

There are many different approaches to working with families. One of those approaches, family problem solving, is discussed in this chapter. This model has been chosen because it is an extension of the problem–solving model for work with individuals, it is consistent with the research about what works, and it has some research support as an effective method for working with involuntary clients.

The model involves the same steps as those involved in problem solving with individuals: problem survey, problem ranking, problem exploration, setting goals, contract, strategies and tasks, and review. Like problem solving with individuals the process should be accompanied by appropriate role clarification, prosocial modelling and reinforcement, and appropriate use of the relationship.

8 | Evaluation

W ORKERS WITH INVOLUNTARY clients derive their knowledge for practice from a variety of sources. These include theories, models, research findings, values and beliefs, experience, and organisational expectations. I have argued in favour of an empirical approach to their direct practice—in other words, an approach which makes use of research findings as a primary source of knowledge for practice. I have suggested that in using an empirical approach, workers should be clear about the purpose of their intervention and the values they wish to encourage.

I have also argued that the use of the practice model presented in this book will increase the likelihood that client and worker goals will be achieved. Empirical practice cannot, however, guarantee that work in any given instance will be successful. It may be that a worker will spend time exploring role with his client, will model and reinforce pro-social expressions, and will work through a client-oriented problem-solving process in a manner which is consistent with what the research says works. Yet despite this the client may not improve. She might abuse her children again, retreat to the use of drugs, be readmitted to hospital or end up in gaol.

An empirical approach has its limitations. Sometimes personal or environmental influences on the client are so strong that the client deteriorates despite the good work of the worker. In other instances the generalised messages from research are insufficient to guide specific interventions. In these instances workers must make individual judgements about how they work with their clients. For example, the research knowledge about when it is appropriate to use confrontation or humour is limited. Getting the balance right between the use of empathy, a focus on pro-social actions and expressions, and challenging rationalisations can also be difficult. Direct practice inevitably requires difficult individual judgements.

In many instances it will not be clear whether a client has made progress in relation to the general presenting problem such as drug use, child abuse or offending. In other instances workers may have this information, but it may relate only to the period of contact rather than over a longer term.

How can a worker know whether a client is improving as a result of the intervention which is being offered?

This chapter outlines two approaches which can assist workers to evaluate their own work, both of which provide some ongoing information to workers about client progress and about their own intervention style. The first approach, single case study evaluation, aims to help workers know if their clients have progressed during their intervention. The second, which I refer to as case analysis, involves workers examining how they have worked with their clients and how they might have done things differently.

It is not within the scope of this book to provide a comprehensive examination of evaluation procedures, and these approaches are dealt with briefly. More has been written elsewhere about single case study research (e.g. Grinnell 1993) and about case analysis and reflective research (e.g. Fook 1996). The aim here is simply to present a few practical strategies which might assist workers evaluate some of their day-to-day work.

SINGLE CASE STUDY EVALUATION

Single case study evaluation involves systematically evaluating the progress of the client against specific objectives through the course of the intervention. It generally involves the client commenting on their progress.

Client evaluations are of course only one measure of effectiveness, and perhaps less persuasive than hard data measures like reoffending, more hospital admissions or further notifications of abuse. Nonetheless, client perspectives have value in their own right. Additionally, some research suggests that positive client evaluations tend to correlate with positive hard data evaluations (LaSala 1997). In other words, clients seem to know if they are being helped.

Single case study evaluations vary in their complexity. At the lowest level, single case study evaluation might involve the worker simply asking the client to rate the extent to which goals and objectives have been achieved. This might involve a review which is little different from the review stage of the problem-solving process. In fact the faithful application of the problem-solving process should provide the worker with considerable information about the progress of the client. The worker and the client should discuss both during and at the conclusion of the intervention the progress the client has made in relation to his goals.

The worker and the client might also discuss the feelings and views of the client about the casework process and the extent to which it has been helpful. The worker might ask the client what other things could have been done or said which might have helped the client more.

It has been my experience that workers with involuntary clients for the most part finish their contact with their clients without taking advantage of the opportunity to talk to them about their experience of the casework process. How did you find this contact? Did it help you? Were there things I might have done differently? The answers to these questions can help workers develop a more effective style of working. In my view it is the very least which might be expected from professional workers. Organisations dealing with involuntary clients would do well to incorporate such practices into their standards documents, practice manuals and report forms.

At the next level of single case study methods, workers might use ongoing evaluation procedures with their clients in relation to general progress and in relation to specific problems. Presented on page 146 are client monitoring forms which were used in my family problem-solving research (Trotter 1997b).

Workers in the family problem-solving research project completed these forms with families at each session. The accumulating forms provided an ongoing assessment by the family of progress in relation to the specific problems which were being addressed, and in relation to general family relationships.

The information from such forms can then be presented on a graph to provide a more visual demonstration of the client's progress in relation to the particular issues which have been measured. An example is shown in Figure 8.1. (Note that this type of evaluation can of course be used in direct practice with individuals as well as families.)

Rating scale for families

To be completed by the workers or family members at each session. One rating scale should be completed by each family member.

Circle a number on the scale 1 to 5 that corresponds to how you feel about the problem.

1   2   3   4   5

1. The problem is very serious and makes it very difficult to cope with everyday life.
2. The problem is very serious but you are able to cope with most everyday tasks.
3. The problem is serious but does not interfere with your everyday life.
4. The problem is not that serious and you are able to cope with it reasonably well.
5. There is no real problem.

General family functioning rating scale

To be completed by worker or family member at each session for each family member.

Circle a number on the scale 1 to 5 that corresponds with how you feel about the family.

1   2   3   4   5

Family relationships in our family at the present time are:

1. Poor, that is continual arguing, people rarely speak to each other, there is virtually no communication other than to dispute things.
2. Unsatisfactory, that is there is some positive communication between at least some family members, however overall family relationships are problematic and/or unsatisfying.
3. Satisfactory, that is family members communicate on some issues and there is some satisfaction in family life although things could be a lot better.
4. Very satisfactory, that is basically things are OK within the family and family members generally communicate without too much problem. Things still could be better however.
5. Good, that is family life is not characterised by arguments or poor communication and family members find it generally satisfying.

Figure 8.1 **Client assessment of family functioning over a ten-week intervention**

Family relationships scale										
Week	1	2	3	4	5	6	7	8	9	10
5								*	*	*
4					*	*	*			
3					*	*	*			
2				*						
1	*	*	*							

This type of single case study evaluation can of course also be used with hard data measures, such as school attendance.

This level of single case study evaluation is relatively easy to administer, takes only a few minutes, in no way compromises the casework process and provides ongoing information about the client's progress. It does not, however, inform the worker about the extent to which any changes in the client's situation relate to the direct practice intervention. It could be that the client or family members would have improved anyway.

More sophisticated (high-level) single case study techniques do attempt to provide information about the extent to which the worker has contributed to the improvement. These generally involve a higher level of intrusion into the direct practice process. For example, the client's situation might be monitored over a period of time before any intervention is offered. This might involve delaying intervention and interviewing the client about the situation a number of times before casework begins. This at least provides a more meaningful assessment of the original problem against which progress can be compared. Other single case study designs withdraw services for a period of time to assess whether there is some deterioration in the client's progress. If the intervention is contributing to the client's progress then presumably the progress would be affected by the worker's temporary withdrawal.

These higher-level single case study designs have obvious practical, if not ethical, problems for most workers with involuntary clients. For the most part workers are required to deliver services immediately and continuously. The use of higher-level single case study designs has been controversial for this and for other reasons. They have been criticised because workers are reluctant to use them, they do not benefit clients and the results are difficult to interpret (Rubin & Knox 1996). Nonetheless, there is a vast literature on single case study designs and practices of all types, particularly in the United States, where the use of single case study practices has been associated with professional accreditation of social workers.

To sum up, I believe there is a strong argument for workers to routinely seek the opinions of their clients about their progress and about the extent to which the worker is helping. Low- and medium-level single case study evaluations can help to provide this and can provide a valuable supplement to empirical practice as it has been defined in this book.

CASE ANALYSIS

Another method by which workers can evaluate their own practice is through case analysis. For the purposes of this discussion case analysis involves analysing the way a worker is working or has worked with a particular client or client family. It involves reflecting upon and analysing the extent to which the work is consistent with research about what works and about the sources of knowledge which have been drawn upon by the worker.

Outlined below are a series of questions which workers might address in an attempt to analyse the extent to which their work is consistent with empirical practice. These questions might also be used in supervision sessions by senior workers to help their staff examine the casework process. The use of similar questions in an exploratory study in a mental health setting resulted in more use of 'effective' practices by workers and higher levels of satisfaction by clients (Harkness & Hensley 1991). If workers can give clear and positive answers to these questions they are likely to be doing effective work with their clients.

1. What does/do the client/s understand to be the purpose of your work with them?
2. What have you done to reach agreement with your client/s about purpose?
3. What does/do your client/s hope to achieve from this intervention?
4. Are you working with your client's objectives?
5. How will you know if the client is successful in achieving his/her objectives?
6. Has the client suggested strategies to achieve the objectives?

7. Do you have a contract?
8. What positive comments/actions did you praise or reward in your last interview?
9. Did the rewards or praise you offered substantially outnumber the instances of confrontation or critical comments?
10. What actions/comments did you confront or criticise in your last interview?
11. Does the client believe you are helping?

The worker might also reflect upon the extent to which various factors such as values, research findings, organisational expectations, theories or personal experiences have influenced the way he worked with the client. The worker might also ask himself:

- What sources of information have I used in my work with this client (e.g. research findings, values, organisational expectations, theories)?
- Why and how have I used these?

Critical incidents

A second approach to the analysis of cases, besides analysing the work with a client, involves critical incidents. Critical incidents can be defined in different ways. The following definition makes use of work by Martin Ryan et al. (1995) and Jan Fook (1996). A critical incident relates to a situation which seemed to help the client a lot; which seemed to be most *un*helpful to the client; which the worker found very difficult and caused a lot of anxiety; which gave the worker a great deal of satisfaction; which led to a realisation about the nature of the work; which challenged the worker's beliefs; or which left the worker confused about what he was doing.

Workers might examine critical incidents in terms of why they were critical and how they felt about them at the time. They might also consider:

- What knowledge, values, experiences or expectations did you take into account in responding to the situation?
- Are there research findings or is there other knowledge which might have helped you deal with the situation better?
- To what extent was your handling of the incident consistent with research about effective casework practice? Were there, for example, issues relating to role clarification, the values or

practices you reinforced, or about the extent to which you focused on the client's definition of the problem?

- How would you handle the incident differently if you were in a similar situation again?

These questions might be worked through individually, with a colleague or in supervision.

Case analysis using these sorts of questions can help the worker to evaluate their practice and consider how it can be more effective. It complements the lower level single case study analysis which helps workers become more effective by monitoring client progress. These approaches in turn complement the use of research-based or empirical approaches to work with involuntary clients.

CONCLUSION

It was pointed out in Chapter 1 that workers with involuntary clients, like others in the welfare sector, for the most part do not make use of research or theory in their work (e.g. Carew 1979; Ryan et al. 1995).

The reasons for this are open to speculation. In my own work in probation and child protection, and in brief stints in mental health and in drug rehabilitation, I felt for many years after my graduation in social work that I was working in a theoretical vacuum. It was not that I did not wish to use research findings or theory in my work, it was simply that I was confused about what research findings to use and how to use them. What I learned in a university social work course somehow did not translate into my practice with involuntary clients.

As the state of knowledge about effective practices developed through the 1980s and 1990s it became apparent that some practices worked better with involuntary clients than others (e.g. Rubin 1985; Videka Sherman 1988; Andrews et al. 1990; Shulman 1991; Reid 1997a). Even though workers tended not to consciously use research or theory some workers seemed to be more inclined to use effective practices than others.

It was in this context that I undertook a study in probation in Victoria, Australia, with a view to presenting a user-friendly research-based direct practice model to a group of probation officers, and encouraging those officers to make use of the model. It was apparent that the probation officers involved did consciously make use of the model and their clients did benefit. In fact they went to prison about half as often as other clients in the study (Trotter 1996a).

In this book I have tried to present a practice model which is soundly based on research findings but which takes into account other important sources of knowledge, particularly the values of the worker. I have tried to present it in a way which is jargon-free and accessible to the wide range of people who work with involuntary clients.

It is my hope that this book will influence the practice of those people. And it is my hope that in turn something of the day-to-day pain and suffering, which is the norm for so many of our clients, will be alleviated.

Appendix: Principles of effective practice

This summary of the principles of effective practice is designed to be displayed in the offices of workers who use this model and to be shared with clients. It aims to provide a reminder to workers about effective practices and to help familiarise clients with the approach of their worker.

1. ROLE CLARIFICATION

Involves frequent open and honest discussions about role, for example:

- the purpose of your intervention;
- your dual role as helper/investigator;
- the client's expectations of you;
- your authority and how it can be used;
- negotiable and non-negotiable areas;
- confidentiality (or who can know).

2. PRO-SOCIAL MODELLING AND REINFORCEMENT

- Identify behaviours/comments you wish to promote.
- Reward/encourage the comments/behaviours you wish to promote.
- Model the behaviour/comments you wish to promote.
- Identify and discourage or confront comments/behaviours you wish to change.
- Aim for four positives or rewards to every negative or confrontational comment.

3. PROBLEM SOLVING

- Problem survey.
- Problem ranking.
- Problem exploration.
- Setting goals.
- Developing a contract.
- Developing strategies.
- Ongoing monitoring.

4. RELATIONSHIP

The worker should:

- be open and honest;
- use empathy;
- challenge rationalisations, not minimise;
- be non-blaming;
- be optimistic;
- articulate client and family members' feelings and problems;
- use appropriate self-disclosure;
- use appropriate humour.

Note: For seminars or videos on working with involuntary clients Dr Chris Trotter can be contacted at the Social Work Department, Monash University, Clayton, 3168, Australia.

Bibliography

Acierno, R., Donohue, B. & Kogan, E. (1994) 'Psychological interventions for drug abuse: a critique and summation of controlled studies', *Clinical Psychology Review* 14:417–42

Akers, R.L. (1994) *Criminological Theories—Introduction and Evaluation,* Roxbury Publishing, Los Angeles, California

Alexander, J., Barton, C., Shiavo, R.S. & Parsons, B.V. (1978) 'Systems behavioural intervention with families of delinquents: therapist characteristics, family behaviour and outcome', *Journal of Consulting and Clinical Psychology* 44:656–64

Alexander, J. & Parsons, B.V. (1973) 'Short-term behavioural intervention with delinquent families: impact on family process and recidivism' *Journal of Consulting and Clinical Psychology* 81:219–25

——(1982) *Functional Family Therapy,* Brooks Cole, Monterey, California

Anderson, S.C. & Mandell, D.L. (1989) 'The use of self-disclosure by professional social workers', *Social Casework* 70:5:259–67

Andrews, D.A. (1982) *The Level of Supervision Inventory,* Carleton University, Ottawa

Andrews, D.A. & Bonta, J. (1994) *The Psychology of Criminal Conduct,* Anderson Publishing, Cincinnati

Andrews, D.A., Keissling, J.J. & Robinson, D. (1986) 'The risk principle of case classification: an outcome evaluation with young adult probationers', *Canadian Journal of Criminology* 28:4:377–84

Andrews, D.A., Keissling, J.J., Russell, R.J. & Grant, B.A. (1979) *Volunteers and the One-to-One Supervision of Adult Probationers,* Ontario Ministry of Correctional Services, Toronto

Andrews, D.A. & Robinson, D. (1984) *The Level of Supervision Inventory: Second Report,* Ontario Ministry of Correctional Services, Ottawa

Andrews, D.A., Zinger, I., Hoge, R., Bonta, J., Gendreau, P. & Cullen, F. (1990) 'Does correctional treatment work? A clinically relevant and psychologically informed meta-analysis', *Criminology* 28:3:369–401

Annis, H.M. (1990) 'Effective treatment for drug and alcohol problems: what do we know?', *Forum on Corrections Research* 2:4:18–24

Armstrong, J. (1994) 'An approach to lighten and enlighten social work practice: the role of humour in counselling', unpublished paper, Dept of Social Work, Monash University, Melbourne

Bandura, A. (1977) 'Self-efficacy: towards a unifying theory of behavioural change', *Psychological Review* 84:191–215

Barber, J. (1991) *Beyond Casework*, Macmillan, Basingstoke

——(1995) 'Working with resistant drug abusers', *Social Work* 40:1:17–23

Barton, C. & Alexander, J. (1981) 'Functional family therapy' in *Handbook of Family Therapy*, eds A.S. Gurman & P. Kniskern, Brunner Mayel, New York

Barton, C., Alexander, J.F., Waldron, H., Turner, C.W. & Warburton, J. (1985) 'Generalising treatment effects of functional family therapy: three replications', *American Journal of Family Therapy* 13:16–26

Benjamin, J., Bessant, J., Watts, R. (1997) *Making Groups Work*, Allen & Unwin, Sydney

Berg, I.K. (1994) *Family-based Practice—a Solution-focussed Approach*, W.W. Norton, New York

Berg, I.K. & DeJong, P. (1996) 'Solution-building conversations: Co-constructuring a sense of competence with clients', *Families in Society* 77:6:376–91

Bergman, A., Wells, L., Bogo, M., Abbey, S., Chandler, V., Embleton, L., Guirgis, S., Huot, A., McNeill, T., Prentice, L., Stapleton, D., Shekter-Woldson & Urman, S. (1993) 'High risk indicators for family involvement in social work in health care: a review of the literature', *Social Work* 38:3:281–96

Bowie, V. (1996) *Coping with Violence—A Guide for the Human Services*, 2nd edn, Whiting & Birch, London

Braithwaite, J. (1992) *Violence: Understanding, Intervention and Prevention*, Radcliffe Professional Press, Oxford

Briar, S. (1990) 'Empiricism in clinical practice' in *Advances in Clinical Social Work Practice*, eds L. Videka Sherman & W. Reid, National Association of Social Workers Press, Baltimore

Brown, A. (1992) *Groupwork*, 3rd edn, Arena, Aldershot

Brown, K.O., Saunders, D.C. & Staeker, K.M. (1997) 'Process-psychodynamic groups for men who batter: a brief treatment model', *Families in Society* 78:2:265–71

Burns, P. (1994) Pro-social Practices in Community Corrections, honours thesis, Monash University, Dept of Social Work, Melbourne

Carew, R. (1979) 'The place of knowledge in social work activity', *British Journal of Social Work* 9:349–93

Carkhuff, R.R. (1969) *Helping and Human Relations*, Holt Rinehart & Winston, New York

Compton, B. & Galaway, B. (1994) *Social Work Processes*, 5th edn, Dorsey, Homewood

DeChillo, N. (1993) 'Collaboration between social workers and families of patients with mental illness', *Families in Society* 74:2:104–15

DeJong, P. & Miller, S. (1996) 'How to interview for client strengths', *Social Work* 40:6:729–36

Derlega, V.J. & Berg, J.H. (1987) *Self-Disclosure: Theory Research and Therapy*, Plenum Press, New York

DeShazer, S. (1988) *Clues: Investigating Solutions in Brief Therapy*, W.W. Norton, New York

Doel, M. & Marsh, P. (1992) *Task-centred Social Work*, Ashgate, Aldershot

Dungee-Anderson, D. & Beckett, J. (1995) 'A process model for multi-cultural social work practice', *Families in Society* 76:8:459–68

Edleson, J. & Syers, M. (1990) 'Relative effectiveness of group treatment for men who batter', *Social Work Research and Abstracts* 26:2:10–17

Edmund, M. (1991) 'Brief casework: effectiveness, methods and values', *Australian Social Work* 43:2:3–11

Epstein, N.B. & Bishop, D.S. (1981) 'Problem-centred systems and the family' in *Handbook of Family Therapy*, eds A.S. Gurman & P. Kniskern, Brunner Mayel, New York

Ferguson, J.E. (1983) 'A neo-Lewinian approach to the identification of mechanisms of change in research with offenders', unpublished PhD thesis, Carleton University, Ottawa

Fischer, J. (1973) 'Is casework effective—a review', *Social Work* 18:5–20

——(1981) 'The Social Work Revolution', *Social Work* 26:3:199–207

Fo, W. & O'Donnell, C. (1974) 'The buddy system: relationship and contingency conditions in a community intervention program for youth with non-professionals as charge agents', *Journal of Consulting and Clinical Psychology*, 42:163–69

Fook, J. (1986) 'Feminist contributions to casework practice' in *Gender Reclaimed*, eds H. Marchant & B. Wearing, Hale & Iremonger, Sydney

——(1993) *Radical Casework*, Allen & Unwin, Sydney

——ed. (1996) *The Reflective Researcher*, Allen & Unwin, Sydney

Forgatch, M. & Patterson, G. (1989) *Parents and Adolescents Living Together: Part 1 The Basics; Part 2 Family Problem Solving*, Castalia Publishing, Eugene, Oregon

Fortune, A. (1992) 'Inadequate resources' in *Task Strategies: An Empirical Approach to Clinical Social Work*, ed. W. Reid, Columbia University Press, New York

Furstenberg, A.L. & Rounds, K.A. (1995) 'Self-efficacy as a target for social work intervention', *Families in Society* 6:9:587–95

Gambrill, E. (1994) 'What's in a name: task-centred empirical and behavioural practice', *Social Service Review*, 68:4:578–99

Garvin, C. (1992) 'A task-centred group approach to work with the mentally ill', *Social Work with Groups* 15:1:67–80

Gendreau, P. (1996) 'The principles of effective intervention with offenders in Harland AT' (ed) *Choosing Correctional Options that Work*, Sage Publications, Newbury Park, California

Germain, C.B. & Gitterman, A. (1996) *The Life Model of Social Work Practice: Advances in Theory and Practice*, Columbia University Press, New York

Gingerich, S.L. & Bellack, A.S. (1996) 'Research-based family interventions for the treatment of schizophrenia', *Research on Social Work Practice* 6:1:122–26

Goldstein, E. (1995) *Ego Psychology and Social Work Practice*, 2nd edn, Free Press, New York

Gordon, D.A. & Arbuthnot, J. (1990) 'Promising approaches for chronic juvenile offenders: interventions with the family and other social systems', paper presented at the annual convention of the American Society of Criminology, Baltimore

Gordon, D.A., Arbuthnot, J., Gustafson, K.E. & McGreen, P. (1988) 'Home-based behavioural systems: family therapy with disadvantaged juvenile delinquents', *American Journal of Family Therapy* 16:3:243–55

Gottschalk, L. (1973) 'A study of prediction and outcome in a mental health crisis clinic', *American Journal of Psychiatry* 130:1107–11

Gough, D. (1993) *Child Abuse Interventions—A Review of the Research Literature*, Public Health Research Unit, University of Glasgow, HMSO, London

Gough, H.G. (1960) 'Theory and measurement of socialisation', *Journal of Consulting Psychology* 24:1:23–30

Grinnell, R.M. (1993) *Social Work Research and Evaluation*, F.E. Peacock, Itasca, Illinois

Harkness, D. & Hensley, H. (1991) 'Changing the focus of social work supervision: effects on client satisfaction and generalised contentment', *Social Work* 36:6:506–12

Heffernan, J., Shuttlesworth, G. & Ambrosino, R. (1997) *Social Work and Social Welfare: An Introduction*, West Publishing Company, New York

Hepworth, D.H., Rooney, R.R. & Larson, J.A. (1997) *Direct Social Work Practice*, Brooks Cole, Pacific Grove, California

HMSO (1995) *Child Protection—Messages From Research*, HMSO, London

Hogan, R. (1969) 'Development of an empathy scale', *Journal of Consulting Psychology* 34:3:307–16

Horne, A. & Passmore, L. (1991) *Family Counselling and Therapy*, F.E. Peacock, Itasca, Illinois

Hough, G. (1994) 'Post industrial work: the use of information technology in the restructuring of state social service work', *Advances in Social Work and Welfare Education*, University of Western Australia, Perth

——(1996) 'Using ethnographic methods to research the work world of social workers in child protection' in *The Reflective Researcher*, ed. J. Fook, Allen & Unwin, Sydney

Hudson, B.L. & McDonald, G.M. (1986) *Behavioural Social Work: An Introduction*, Macmillan, London

Ife, J. (1997) *Rethinking Social Work*, Longman, Melbourne

Ivanoff, A., Blythe, B. & Tripodi, T. (1994) *Involuntary Clients in Social Work Practice*, Aldine de Gruyter, New York

Ivanoff, A., Robinson, E. & Blythe, B. (1987) 'Empirical clinical practice from a feminist perspective', *Social Work* 32:417–23

Jones, J.A. & Alcabes, A. (1993) *Client Socialisation: The Achilles Heel of the Helping Professions*, Auburn House, Wesport, Connecticut

Keissling, J.J. (1982) *The Problem Solving Dimension in Correctional Counselling*, Ontario Ministry of Correctional Services, Ottawa

Kirk, S.A. & Koeske, G.F. (1995) 'The fate of optimism: a longitudinal study of case managers' hopefulness and subsequent morale', *Research on Social Work Practice* 5:1:47–61

Lambert, M., Shapiro, D. & Bergin, A. (1986) 'The effectiveness of psychotherapy' in *Psychotherapy and Behaviour Change*, 3rd edn, eds S.L. Garfield & A.E. Bergin, Wiley, New York

LaSala, M. (1997) 'Client satisfaction: consideration of correlates and response bias', *Families in Society* 78:1:54–62

Lipsey, M.W. (1992) 'Juvenile delinquency treatment: a meta-analytic inquiry into the variability of effects' in T.D. Cook et al., *Meta-Analysis for Explanation: A Casebook*, Russell Sage Foundation, New York

Loneck, B. (1995) 'Getting persons with alcohol and other drug problems into treatment: teaching the Johnson intervention in the practice curriculum', *Journal of Teaching in Social Work* 11:(1–2):31–44

Lunden, R. (1989) 'Parole release and discharge from prison: a comparison study', Massachusetts Parole Board, paper presented to the American Society of Criminology Conference, November

Lyons, P., Doueck, H. & Wodarski, J. (1996) 'Risk assessment for child protective services: a review of the empirical literature on instrument performance', *Social Work Research* 20:3:143–55

Marchant, H. & Wearing, B. eds (1986) *Gender Reclaimed: Women in Social Work*, Hale & Iremonger, Sydney

Markiewicz, A. (1994) 'How social workers survive in public welfare: training for best practice in a declassified, increasingly narrowly administrative context', *Advances in Social and Welfare Education*, University of Western Australia, Perth

Marlowe, H., Reid, J.B., Patterson, G.R. & Weinrott, M. (1989) 'Treating adolescent multiple offenders: a comparison and follow-up of parent training for families of chronic delinquents', unpublished paper cited in Andrews, D.A. & Bonta, J. (1994)

Marziali, E. & Alexander, L. (1991) 'The power of the therapeutic relationship', *American Journal of Orthopsychiatry* 61:3:383–91

Masters, J., Thomas, G., Hollon, S. & Rimm, D. (1987) *Behaviour Therapy*, Harcourt Brace, Fort Worth, Florida

McIvor, G. (1992) *Sentenced to Serve*, Avebury, London

McQuaide, S. & Ehrenreich, J. (1997) 'Assessing client strengths', *Families in Society* 78:2:201–12

McPherson, L., McNamara, N. & Hemsworth, C. (1997) 'A model for multi-disciplinary collaboration in child protection', *Children Australia* 22:1:21–8

Milgram, D. & Rubin, J. (1992) 'Resisting resistance; involuntary substance abuse group therapy', *Social Work with Groups* 15:1:95–110

Miller, P., Herson, M., Eisler, R. & Watts, J. (1974) 'Contingent reinforcement of lowered blood/alcohol levels in an outpatient chronic alcoholic', *Behaviour Research and Therapy* 12:261–63

Moore, K.J., Greenfield, W.L., Wilson, M. & Kok, A. (1997) 'Toward a taxonomy of batterers', *Families in Society* 78:6:353–60

Moore, S. (1992) 'Case management and the integration of services: how service delivery systems shape case management', *Social Work* 37:5:418–23

Mullender, A. (1996) *Rethinking Domestic Violence*, Routledge, London

Murdach, A.D. (1996) 'Beneficence re-examined: protective intervention in mental health', *Social Work* 41:1:26–32

Newhill, C.E. (1996) 'Prevalence and risk factors for client violence towards social workers', *Families in Society* 77:8:488–96

Nugent, W.R. & Halvorson, H. (1995) 'Testing the effects of active listening', *Research on Social Work Practice* 5:2:152–75

O'Connor, I., Wilson, J. & Setterlund, D. (1995) *Social Work and Welfare Practice*, Longman, Melbourne

——(1996) 'Readiness for change: variation by intensity and domain of client distress', *Social Work Research* 20:1:13–18

O'Hare, T. (1991) 'Integrating research and practice: a framework for implementation', *Social Work* 36:3:220–23

Orton, J. & Rich, L. (1988) 'A model for assessment of incestuous families', *Social Casework*, 69:611–20

Owen, L. & Richards, D. (1995) 'Social work and corrections' in *In the Shadow of the Law*, ed. P. Swain, Federation Press, Sydney

Perlman, H.H. (1957) *Social Casework: A Problem Solving Process*, University of Chicago Press, Chicago

Pollio, D.E. (1995) 'Use of humour in crisis intervention', *Families in Society* 76:6:376–84

Puckett, T.C. & Cleak, H. (1994) 'Caution—helping may be hazardous: client abuse, threats and assaults', *Australian Social Work* 47:1:3–10

Raynor, P. & Vanstone, M. (1996) 'Reasoning and rehabilitation in Britain: the results of the Straight Thinking on Probation (STOP) programme', *International Journal of Offender Therapy and Comparative Criminology* 40:4:272–84

Reid, W. (1985) *Family Problem Solving*, Columbia University Press, New York

———ed. (1992) *Task Strategies: An Empirical Approach to Clinical Social Work*, Columbia University Press, New York

———(1994) 'The empirical practice movement', *Social Service Review* 68:2:163–84

———(1997a) 'Evaluating the dodo's verdict. Do all interventions have equivalent outcomes?', *Social Work Research* 21:1:5–16

———(1997b) 'Research on task-centred practice', *Social Work Research* 21:3:134–37

Reid, W. & Epstein, L. (1972) *Task-centred Casework*, Columbia University Press, New York

Reid, W. & Hanrahan, P. (1982) 'Recent evaluations of social work: grounds for optimism', *Social Work* 27:328–40

———eds (1997) *Task Centred Practice*, Columbia University Press, New York

Reid, W. & Shyne, A. (1969) *Brief and Extended Casework*, Columbia University Press, New York

Rey, L.D. (1996) 'What social workers need to know about client violence', *Families in Society* 77:1:33–39

Roberts, C. (1993) 'What works—using social work methods to reduce reoffending in serious and persistent offenders', Social Work Department, Oxford University, Oxford

Rogers, C. (1942) *Counselling and Psychotherapy*, Houghton Mifflin, Boston

Rooney, R. (1992) *Strategies for Work with Involuntary Clients*, Columbia University Press, New York

Rothman, J. (1991) 'A model of case management: toward empirically based practice', *Social Work* 36:6:337–43

Rubin, A. (1985) 'Practice effectiveness: more grounds for optimism', *Social Work* 30:469–76

Rubin, A. & Knox, K. (1996) 'Data analysis problems in single case evaluation: issues for research on social work practice, *Research on Social Work Practice* 6:1:40–65

Russell, M.N. (1990) *Clinical Social Work*, Sage Publications, Newbury Park, California

Ryan, M., Fook, J. & Hawkins, L. (1995) 'From beginner to graduate social worker: preliminary findings of an Australian longitudinal study', *British Journal of Social Work* 25:1:17–35

Sarenson, I.G. & Ganzer, V.J. (1973) 'Modelling and group discussion in the rehabilitation of juvenile delinquents', *Journal of Consulting Psychology* 20:5:442–49

Scott, D. & O'Neill, D. (1996) *Beyond Child Rescue*, Allen & Unwin, Sydney

Seligman, M. (1990) *Learned Optimism*, Random House, Sydney

———(1995) *The Optimistic Child*, Random House, Sydney

Sheldon, B. (1987) 'Implementing findings from social work effectiveness research', *British Journal of Social Work* 17:573–86

Shulman, L. (1991) *Interactional Social Work Practice: Toward an Empirical Theory*, F.E. Peacock, Itasca, Illinois

——(1993) *Interactional Supervision*, National Association of Social Workers, Washington DC

Simons, R.L. (1985) 'Inducement as an approach to exercising influence', *Social Work* 30:1:56–62

Siporin, M. (1984) 'Have you heard the one about social work humour?', *Social Casework* 68:8:459–64

Smokowski, P. & Wodarski, J. (1996) 'Effectiveness of child welfare services', *Research on Social Work Practice* 6:4:504–23

Swain, P. ed. (1995) *In the Shadow of the Law*, Federation Press, Sydney

Thomas, E.J. (1970) 'Behavioural modification and casework' in *Theories of Social Casework*, R. Roberts & R. Nee eds, University of Chicago Press, Chicago

Thomlinson, R. (1984) 'Something works: evidence from practice effectiveness studies', *Social Work* 29:1:51–56

Thorpe, D. (1994) *Evaluating Child Protection*, Open University Press, Buckingham

Trotter, C. (1990) 'Probation can work: a research study using volunteers', *Australian Journal of Social Work* 43:2:13–18

——(1993) 'The effective supervision of offenders', unpublished PhD thesis, La Trobe University, Melbourne

——(1994) 'Task-centred social work—an interview with William Reid', *Advances in Social Work Education* 2:3–5

——(1995a) *The Supervision of Offenders—What Works? First and Second Reports to the Criminology Research Council*, Department of Social Work, Monash University, and Dept of Justice, Victoria, Australia

——(1995b) 'Contamination theory and unpaid community work', *Australian and New Zealand Journal of Criminology* 28:2:163–75

——(1996a) 'The impact of different supervision practices in community corrections', *Australian and New Zealand Journal of Criminology* 29:1:29–46

——(1996b) 'Community corrections—punishment or welfare—a book review essay', *International Criminal Justice Review* 6:121–30

——(1997a) 'Working with mandated clients—a pro-social approach', *Australian Journal of Social Work* 50:2:19–27

——(1997b) *Family Problem Solving—Report to Vic Safe*, Department of Social Work, Monash University, Melbourne

——(1997c) 'Effective interventions in child protection', *Family Violence Research Conference*, University of New Hampshire, Durham, conference paper

Truax, C.B., Wargo, D.G. & Sibler, L.D. (1966) 'Effects of group psychotherapy with high accurate empathy and non-possessive warmth upon female institutionalised delinquents', *Journal of Abnormal Psychology* 71:4:267–74

Turner, F.J. ed. (1986) *Social Work Treatment: Interlocking Theoretical Approaches*, Free Press, New York

Videka Sherman, L. (1988) 'Meta-analysis of research on social work practice in mental health', *Social Work* 33:4:323–38

Waterson, L. & Carnie, J. (1992) 'Assessing child protection risk', *British Journal of Social Work* 22:47–60

White, M. & Epston, D. (1989) *Narrative Means to Therapeutic Ends*, Dulwich Centre Publications, Adelaide

Whitehead, J.T. & Lab, S.P. (1989) 'A meta-analysis of juvenile correctional treatment', *Journal of Research in Crime and Delinquency* 26:3:276–95

Witkin, S.L. (1991) 'Empirical clinical practice: a critical analysis', *Social Work* 36:2:158–65

Wood, C. (1997) 'To know or not to know: a critique of postmodernism in social work practice', *Australian Social Work* 50:3:21–28

Wood, M. (1978) 'Casework effectiveness: a new look at the research evidence', *Social Work* 23:6:437–59

Wynne, L.C. ed. (1988) *The State of the Art in Family Therapy Research*, Family Process Press, New York

Zuravin, S., Orme, J. & Hegar, R. (1994) 'Predicting the severity of child abuse injury using ordinal probit regression', *Social Work Research* 18:3:131–38

Index